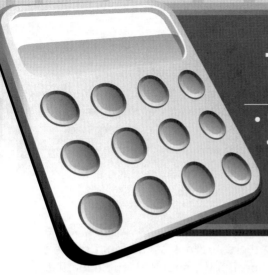

Accounts Receivable Subsystem

- **The Nature of Credit Sales**
- **Designing the Subsystem**
- **Recording and Processing**
- **Accounts Receivable Subsidiary Ledger**
- **Internal Control**

T0359931

The Nature of Credit Sales

This chapter is concerned with accounting for **credit sales**. Sales on credit have become normal practice between businesses in modern times. In order to compete in the marketplace, businesses find that offering credit facilities to customers is an essential aspect of their operations. However, there is always a risk that customers may not pay their accounts, especially when the economic climate is challenging.

Management of customer credit is one of the most important aspects of running a successful business. As far as possible, a business must make sure that only customers who will pay their accounts are allowed to buy goods on credit. Non-payment not only causes the business to suffer losses from bad debts, but also causes problems with cash flow. In some cases this can mean that a business cannot pay its debts. This chapter identifies ways of minimising credit losses.

We will also introduce the **subsidiary ledger** for accounts receivable (called the **accounts receivable ledger**). A subsidiary ledger is a ledger kept *outside* the main accounting records of the business. It contains the detail of a single account in the general ledger. Using a subsidiary ledger for accounts receivable enables the business to keep track of individual customer accounts.

Designing the Subsystem

Previously we learnt that accounting was the 'communication of financial information so that users can make informed decisions'. This financial information is produced by an **accounting system**. A system may be represented as:

Input → (encode) → Process → (decode) → Output

The **input** is the daily transaction record of the business. Transactions are recorded on source documents such as EFTPOS receipts, cheque butts, bank statements invoices, receipts, credit notes etc.

The **process** is the classifying and recording of information in records called journals and ledgers. The information is then summarised in the trial balance.

The **output** is the financial statements – the income statement and statement of financial position.

An accounting system comprises a number of **subsystems,** each of which produces financial information about a specific area of the business. Subsystems exist to account for cash receipts, cash payments, sales and accounts receivable, inventory and accounts payable, payroll, and property, plant and equipment. We met aspects of cash receipts and cash payments subsystems in earlier courses.

Accounting for sales and accounts receivable thus forms *part* of the overall accounting system. When we are designing an accounting subsystem, we must identify first the information that management will require for decision-making. We then start from the end – identify the *output* that will provide the required management information. Some questions that must be answered are:

- What reports do we want the subsystem to produce?
- What information is contained on those reports?
- Where will this information come from?

Once we have decided exactly what the output of the subsystem will be, we can design a process to produce that output. From there, we look at the input phase to identify the data that must be captured and to design the source documents that will capture the data efficiently.

In designing the subsystem, it is helpful to have a list of objectives which we want it to achieve. A suitable statement of objectives could be as follows:

> To operate an accounting system that will:
> - allow the prompt and accurate processing of sales orders
> - record credit transactions accurately through appropriate source documents and journal entries
> - process these transactions in ledger accounts and provide an up-to-date list of accounts receivable
> - provide details of the ageing of debtors
> - produce monthly customer statements
> - provide accurate records of GST liability
> - ensure that all credit notes are properly authorised and issued only in accordance with the firm's policy
> - maintain an adequate internal control system to prevent errors and fraud
> - minimise bad debts through an efficient system of credit control
> - provide relevant and timely information to management for decision-making.

If the subsystem meets all of these objectives, the business will achieve the maximum benefit from selling goods on credit, with the minimum risk.

Once the objectives have been determined, the next step is to list the *outputs* required from the subsystem. This has to be done so that the inputs needed can be identified. It also helps decide on the best process to use to convert the inputs into outputs.

If we examine the objectives given above, we can make a list of outputs required:

- Total debtors (Accounts Receivable Control account in the general ledger)
- Details of each customer's account (accounts receivable ledger)
- Customer statements (from the accounts receivable ledger)
- Details of the age of accounts (from the accounts receivable ledger)
- Customer credit ratings (from our own records and from external sources)
- Details of bad debtors (again, from our own records and from external sources)
- Details of GST owed to the Inland Revenue Department (from the GST account in the general ledger).

We must ensure that all the information we need to produce these outputs is an *input* to the system.

PHOTOCOPYING PROHIBITED

ISBN: 9780170229838

Activities

1 Fully explain why it is necessary for businesses to take the risk of selling goods on credit in the modern business environment.

_____

_____

_____

_____

2 a State why you would carry out a **credit check** before allowing a customer to buy goods on credit and explain why it is important.

_____

_____

_____

_____

b Suggest a way you could carry out this process for a **new** credit customer.

_____

_____

_____

_____

c Suggest a way you could carry out this process for an **existing** credit customer.

_____

_____

_____

_____

_____

3 Give TWO reasons why it is important to encourage debtors to pay their accounts on time.

1. _____

2. _____

4 What do you think is meant by the term 'ageing of debtors'?

_____

_____

_____

_____

Internal Control

It is essential to include **internal controls** in the design of any accounting subsystem.

Internal Controls are....

The methods and procedures which ensure that the business operates in accordance with management policies and achieves its objectives.

There are four objectives of internal control:
- to safeguard the business assets
- to provide accurate and reliable accounting data
- to ensure that management policies are followed
- to encourage efficiency and evaluate performance.

For the **accounts receivable** subsystem, the objectives could be:
- to ensure that goods are sold only to credit-worthy customers
- to ensure that all goods which leave the premises are correctly invoiced
- to ensure that all accounts are paid and that payments are recorded accurately
- to ensure that credit notes are issued only for bona fide (genuine) returns.

How do we achieve internal control?

There are five basic principles to follow in order to achieve internal control:

Principles of Internal Control

- Separation of duties
- Competent personnel
- Proper procedures for authorisation
- Adequate documents and records
- Independent checks on performance

Separation of duties means that no individual employee should be involved in all phases of a single transaction. In a cash receipts subsystem, for example, this means that the person who prepares the cash receipts journal should not be responsible for collecting the cash, because this would provide an opportunity to steal cash and leave it out of the journal. For accounts receivable, the person preparing the invoice for a sale should not be responsible for packing the goods because he or she could send goods to friends without charging for them.

Competent personnel requires that employees are well trained and have a detailed job description. The limits to their authority must also be clearly specified. For accounts receivable, for example, this may mean that credit sales above a certain value need to be authorised by a senior staff member.

Proper procedures for authorisation means that processes are in place to ensure that significant transactions are approved and the business assets are protected. For example, all credit notes must be authorised by a senior staff member to make sure that credit given is in accordance with management policies and also is for goods that were actually purchased from the firm.

ISBN: 9780170229838

Adequate documents and records means, for a manual accounting system, that:

- the documents must be designed so that they capture all the data needed to record the transaction in the accounting system;
- documents are pre-numbered and carbon copies are kept so that all documents can be traced and checked, and false documents would be detected; and
- all blank documents, such as spare invoice books, must be kept securely so that whole books cannot be stolen and used fraudulently.

In a computerised accounting system, document design is fundamental to the construction of the accounting software. One critical feature is that the document cannot be output until all of the required input fields have been completed. For example, unless a customer's details had been entered, the invoice would not be complete and could not be printed, nor would the details enter the ledger. Software is programmed to prevent the issue of false documents by numbering the documents in sequence as they are produced. There are no spare invoice books, so security over blank documents is less of an issue.

There is no need for carbon copies in a computerised system since documents are stored electronically. However a regular, secure backup system is essential to ensure that data are not lost.

Independent checks on performance means that the work of employees is checked from time to time. In a large firm, there is often an internal auditor who carries out these checks. In smaller firms, different methods need to be used. Enforcing staff holidays so that a different person has to step in for a short period is one method. Rotation of duties, where people are assigned different parts of the accounting system (such as moving between accounts receivable and payable) is helpful since staff are unlikely to commit fraud if they know that someone else will be checking their work, and errors are more likely to be identified.

In a computerised accounting system, many of these controls are built into the sales accounting software which reduces the likelihood of errors and fraud. It is very important to understand that internal controls are designed to ensure that a system runs efficiently and are not solely for the purpose of preventing fraud. Simple errors made innocently can also be very costly to businesses and a good system of internal control should prevent, or at least detect, most of those errors.

Internal controls for accounts receivable

This section has provided a brief introduction to subsystems design and internal control. In the following sections, we will examine the input, process and output for the accounts receivable subsystem in detail. At each stage we will examine specific internal controls, and at the end of the unit we will take a full overview of the internal control aspects of accounts receivable.

Remember!

- Internal controls are designed to safeguard business assets, provide accurate and reliable accounting data, ensure management policies are followed, and encourage efficiency and evaluate performance.

- While a good internal control system should detect errors and fraud, it is still possible for two or more employees working together to commit fraud.

- Internal controls are incorporated into an accounting subsystem at the design stage.

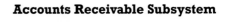

Activities

1 Fully explain how performing a credit check on new customers helps to safeguard business assets.

_____

_____

_____

_____

_____

_____

2 Fully explain how rotating the duties of accounts staff helps to ensure that accounting data are accurate and reliable.

_____

_____

_____

3 Fully explain why invoices in a manual accounting system must be prenumbered in order to:

a safeguard business assets.

_____

_____

_____

_____

_____

b ensure that accounting data are accurate and reliable.

_____

_____

_____

_____

_____

_____

4 Good accounting practice requires that statements showing all transactions for the month are sent to customers at the end of each month. Fully explain how this procedure can help to

a safeguard business assets.

_____

_____

_____

b ensure that accounting data are accurate and reliable.

_____

_____

_____

Accounting – A Next Step

ISBN: 9780170229838

Recording and Processing

Credit Sales

The source document for **credit sales** in a manual accounting system is the carbon copy of a **tax invoice** which has been issued to the customer. The Goods and Services Tax Act 1986 lays down specific requirements for the information to be shown on a tax invoice, depending on the amount involved in the transaction. As well as meeting the requirements of this Act, the invoice must also provide all the information needed by the accounting system of the particular business.

Many large businesses will supply goods only if they receive a **purchase order** from the purchaser. This is a precaution which shows that the firm buying the goods has had the purchase properly authorised and intends to pay for the goods. In large businesses, this process also helps to identify the person who initiated the order and the department to which the purchase is to be charged.

The design of the invoice is very important. It must be easy for the customer to read and also for staff to complete. It must also contain all of the information which is needed by the accounting system of the business. The accurate completion of all source documents is essential because the source document is the point where data is captured to be input into the accounting system.

Examine the tax invoice shown below.

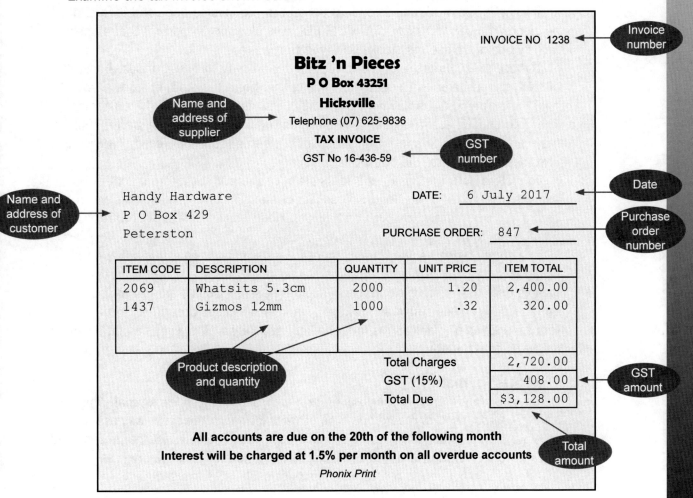

You should note that the invoice contains the following details:

- the name and address of the vendor (supplier) of the goods
- the date of the invoice
- the name and address of the customer (purchaser)
- the invoice number

ISBN: 9780170229838 PHOTOCOPYING PROHIBITED   **Accounts Receivable Subsystem**

- the purchase order number
- a description of the nature, unit cost and quantity of the goods sold.

There are some extra details that are shown for GST purposes:
- the words TAX INVOICE in a prominent place
- the GST registration number of the vendor
- the amount of GST included in the transaction.
    If the total transaction (including GST) is *more* than $1,000:
    - *either* a statement must be made that the total payable includes GST; *or*
    - the amount charged excluding GST, the GST charged and the total payable must all be shown.

    If the total amount of the invoice is *less* than $1,000:
    - A simplified tax invoice may be used for amounts between $50 and $1,000. Purchaser details are **not** required to be shown in this case.
    - For transactions under $50, a tax invoice is not required. Many firms simply stamp the cash register tape with their name and GST number.

Control over Invoices

It is very important that the issue of invoices is well controlled. Invoices are numbered so that every one can be traced. In a manual accounting system, if an invoice is spoilt, all copies should be kept in the invoice book and it should be clearly marked 'VOID' or 'CANCELLED'. It is also very important that all new invoice books are securely locked away until required.

If these procedures are not followed, an opportunity for fraud arises. A member of staff may issue an untraceable invoice (either not numbered, or from a 'spare' book) and intercept the payment from the customer as it arrives. If a customer is known to be careless in checking invoices before paying them, the staff member may continue to do this for some time without being found out, even if no goods have been supplied to the customer.

To protect both the business and its staff, one important internal control is to separate the duties of issuing invoices and opening incoming mail. This control can help prevent activities such as that described above, unless of course two members of staff are colluding with each other.

In a computerised environment, there is less likelihood that this situation would arise. Many customer payments are made electronically which makes it more difficult for staff to intercept incoming cash. Invoices are numbered automatically by the software. However, where a firm uses preprinted invoice forms, supplies of blank forms must be kept securely so that they cannot be stolen and used fraudulently.

The Sales Journal

Credit sales (and only **credit** sales) are first recorded in the **sales journal**. This is a *special journal* used to record one type of transaction, in the same way as a cash receipts journal is used only to record cash received. The sales journal is designed to capture the relevant input into the accounting system from the invoices.

Information needed to record all aspects of each sales transaction is:
- the date of the transaction
- the name of the customer
- the total amount of the invoice
- the GST component of the invoice
- the cost of the goods that were sold.

ISBN: 9780170229838

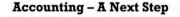

GST – the Invoice Basis

Firms that operate a system of credit journals (i.e. Sales and Purchases journals) are most likely to be registered for GST on the **invoice basis**. This means that the GST is recorded when invoices are sent or received, rather than waiting for the cash to be received or paid.

This is in contrast with the **payments basis** of accounting for GST where GST is recorded only when cash is received or paid. Most businesses using the **payments basis** operate only cash journals and the general journal. They recognise accounts receivable and payable only when they make an adjustment for them at the end of the reporting period.

Time GST recorded	Payments basis	Invoice basis
Cash sale	cash received	cash received
Credit sale	cash received	invoice issued

The invoice basis can cause some cash flow difficulties for businesses which may have to pay the GST to the Inland Revenue Department before they have actually received cash from their customers. On the other hand, they are able to claim GST on invoices from suppliers before they have paid the suppliers' accounts. In this chapter we will use the invoice basis of accounting for GST.

Calculating the Tax Fraction

GST is calculated at the rate of 15%. This represents $^3/_{20}$ ths of the price before GST is added. (We call this the GST *exclusive* price.)

$$\frac{15}{100} = \frac{3}{20}$$

We add $^3/_{20}$ ths of the GST *exclusive* amount to itself to obtain the GST *inclusive* amount. This can be represented by the diagram below.

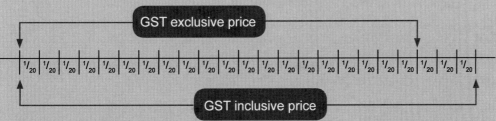

The GST *inclusive* amount is thus $^{23}/_{20}$ ths of the GST *exclusive* amount. In other words, the GST component is $^3/_{23}$ rds of the total price. We can also calculate the GST component of a GST inclusive selling price by dividing by 1.15.

Example:
The GST inclusive selling price is $460.

$$\text{GST component} = \frac{3}{23} \times \$460 \qquad OR \qquad \text{GST component} = \frac{\$460}{1.15}$$

$$= \$60 \qquad\qquad\qquad\qquad = \$60$$

Remember!

When the invoice basis is used, GST is recorded in full immediately when
- an invoice is sent or received; or
- cash is received or paid

whichever occurs first.

The Perpetual Inventory System

In previous courses, inventory was recorded using the **periodic inventory system**. Under this system, the cost of goods sold was calculated at the end of the reporting period by taking opening inventory, adding purchases and other relevant expenses, and then deducting closing inventory. The value of the inventory at year-end was calculated using a physical count of inventory on hand.

In this course we will use a new system of recording inventory – the **perpetual inventory system**. Under this system, a continuous record of inventory on hand is maintained. When inventory is purchased, it is recorded as an **asset**. When inventory is sold, its cost is transferred to the **cost of goods sold** expense.

Consider the following example:

Kiri's Krafts had the following credit sales in September 2019:

Date	Customer Name	Invoice No	Selling price $	Cost price $
Sep 1	Rotorua Souvenirs	201	2,300	940
8	Kerikeri Store	202	1,725	1,080
12	Te Anau Travel	203	1,150	645
14	Hikurangi House	205	276	120
16	Kerikeri Store	206	184	95
20	Rotorua Souvenirs	207	92	40
22	Colinette's Crafts	208	1,840	1,225
25	Te Anau Travel	209	345	180

> **Note**
>
> Invoice 204 was issued for something else so does not appear here.

These are recorded in the sales journal as follows:

Kiri's Krafts							
Sales Journal							**Page 1**
Date	Particulars	Invoice No	Ref	Total $	Sales $	GST $	Cost of goods sold $
Sep 1	Rotorua Souvenirs	201		2,300	2,000	300	940
8	Kerikeri Store	202		1,725	1,500	225	1,080
12	Te Anau Travel	203		1,150	1,000	150	645
14	Hikurangi House	205		276	240	36	120
16	Kerikeri Store	206		184	160	24	95
20	Rotorua Souvenirs	207		92	80	12	40
22	Colinette's Crafts	208		1,840	1,600	240	1,225
25	Te Anau Travel	209		345	300	45	180
				$7,912	$6,880	$1,032	$4,325

Important!

- The sales journal records the credit sale of **goods**. Credit sales of other items, eg property, plant and equipment, are recorded in the general journal.

- The source documents for preparing the sales journal in a manual system are the:
  - carbon copy of the invoice (sale price)
  - inventory stock card (cost of goods sold).

- The sales journal records only **credit** sales. Cash sales are recorded in the *cash receipts* journal.

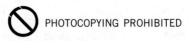 PHOTOCOPYING PROHIBITED

ISBN: 9780170229838

Posting to the Ledger

When using the perpetual inventory system, there are two aspects of sales transactions that must be recorded:

- the sale of goods to the customer
- the cost of the goods that were sold.

We can represent these on the accounting equation as follows:

Recording sales

	A Accounts receivable	+	Ex	=	L GST payable	+	Eq	+	I Sales
Invoices issued $7,912	+ 7,912			=	+ 1,032				+ 6,880
	Debit				**Credit**				**Credit**

Ledger postings require the following entries:

Debit entries	$	Credit entries	$
Accounts receivable	7,912	GST payable	1,032
		Sales	6,880
	$7,912		$7,912

GST!

GST of $1,032 has been invoiced. This must be paid to IRD later.

The relevant accounts in the general ledger, after these entries have been posted, appear as follows: (3-column ledger accounts are on the next page.)

Kiri's Krafts
General Ledger

Accounts receivable   120

Date	Particulars	Ref	$	Date	Particulars	Ref	$
Sep 1	Balance	b/d	6,900				
30	**Sales and GST**	SJ1	**7,912**				

GST payable   310

Date	Particulars	Ref	$	Date	Particulars	Ref	$
				Sep 1	Balance	b/d	1,200
				30	**Accounts**		
					receivable	SJ1	**1,032**

Sales   610

Date	Particulars	Ref	$	Date	Particulars	Ref	$
				Sep 1	Balance	b/d	35,000
				30	**Accounts**		
					receivable	SJ1	**6,880**

Important!

- The posting reference in the ledger accounts is 'SJ1'. This stands for 'Sales Journal, Page 1'.

- There is only one posting for the month, so the date shown is the last day of the month.

Accounts Receivable Subsystem

ISBN: 9780170229838

Kiri's Krafts
General Ledger

Accounts receivable   120

Date	Particulars	Ref	Dr $	Cr $	Balance $
Sep 1	Balance	b/d			6,900 Dr
30	**Sales and GST**	**SJ1**	**7,912**		14,812 Dr

GST payable   310

Date	Particulars	Ref	Dr $	Cr $	Balance $
Sep 1	Balance	b/d			1,200 Cr
30	**Accounts receivable**	**SJ1**		**1,032**	2,232 Cr

Sales   610

Date	Particulars	Ref	Dr $	Cr $	Balance $
Sep 1	Balance	b/d			35,000 Cr
30	**Accounts receivable**	**SJ1**		**6,880**	41,880 Cr

Recording inventory sold

	A	+	Ex	=	L	+	Eq	+	I
	Inventory		Cost of goods sold						

Cost of inventory sold, $4,325 — 4,325 (Credit) + 4,325 (Debit)

NO GST!

GST was accounted for when the goods were originally purchased.

Ledger postings require the following entries:

Debit entries	$	Credit entries	$
Cost of goods sold	4,325	Inventory	4,325

The relevant accounts in the general ledger, after these entries have been posted, appear as follows:

Kiri's Krafts
General Ledger

Inventory   130

Date	Particulars	Ref	$	Date	Particulars	Ref	$
Sep 1	Balance	b/d	6,500	30	Cost of goods sold	SJ1	4,325

Cost of goods sold   710

Date	Particulars	Ref	$	Date	Particulars	Ref	$
Sep 1	Balance	b/d	26,150				
30	**Inventory**	**SJ1**	**4,325**				

 PHOTOCOPYING PROHIBITED

ISBN: 9780170229838

14

In 3-column format, the accounts appear as follows:

Kiri's Krafts
General Ledger

Inventory 130

Date	Particulars	Ref	Dr $	Cr $	Balance $
Sep 1	Balance	b/d			6,500 Dr
30	Cost of goods sold	SJ1		4,325	2,175 Dr

Cost of goods sold 710

Date	Particulars	Ref	Dr $	Cr $	Balance $
Sep 1	Balance	b/d			26,150 Dr
30	Inventory	SJ1	4,325		30,475 Dr

After posting has been completed, the sales journal appears as follows:

	Kiri's Krafts Sales Journal						
Date	Particulars	Invoice No	Ref	Total $	Sales $	GST $	Cost of goods sold $
Sep 1	Rotorua Souvenirs	201		2,300	2,000	300	940
8	Kerikeri Store	202		1,725	1,500	225	1,080
12	Te Anau Travel	203		1,150	1,000	150	645
14	Hikurangi House	205		276	240	36	120
16	Kerikeri Store	206		184	160	24	95
20	Rotorua Souvenirs	207		92	80	12	40
22	Colinette's Crafts	208		1,840	1,600	240	1,225
25	Te Anau Travel	209		345	300	45	180
				$7,912	$6,880	$1,032	$4,325
				120	610	310	710/130

(Page 1)

Important!

- The posting reference for each column is shown below the total. In the cost of goods sold column, the reference (710/130) means that account 710 (cost of goods sold) is to be debited and account 130 (inventory) is to be credited.

- No entries are to be made in the reference column at this stage. This column is used for posting to individual debtor's accounts which we will do later in the chapter.

Activities

1 Complete the following table to show sales income and GST payable for invoices issued:

	Invoice amount $	Sales income $	GST payable $
a	3,680		
b	276		
c	1,541		
d		9,680	
e		950	
f		66,580	
g			3.90
h			21
i			243

2 *Greener Gifts* is registered for GST on the invoice basis. The following balances were extracted from the ledger at 1 August 2018:

Accounts receivable	$7,200 Dr	Sales	$29,500 Cr
Inventory	22,650 Dr	GST payable	960 Cr
Cost of goods sold	16,200 Dr		

The following transactions occurred during the month of August:

Aug 3   Sold goods for $368 to A Carter, Invoice 348, cost of goods sold $210
    8   G Robeson bought goods for $2,070, Invoice 349, cost of goods sold $1,375
   10   Sold goods to I Leavitt, $1,035, Invoice 350, cost of goods sold $715
   11   Cash sales, $920, cost of goods sold $630
   15   P Atapo bought goods for $414, Invoice 351, cost of goods sold $290
   20   T Ancell bought goods for $2,300, Invoice 352, cost of goods sold $1,860
   24   Sold old equipment which had a book value of $320 on credit to A Trader for $506, Invoice 353
   26   Sold goods to B Mere, $138, Invoice 354, cost of goods sold $80.

DO THIS!

a Identify any transactions from the above list that would not appear in the sales journal.
b State where each of the transactions you identified above would be recorded and explain in each case why they are not in the sales journal.
c Prepare the sales journal for *Greener Gifts*.
d Post the journal to the ledger accounts provided. (The chart of accounts references are given on the ledger accounts.)

a Identify any transactions from the above list that would not appear in the sales journal.

_____

_____

b State where each of the transactions you identified above would be recorded and explain in each case why they are not in the sales journal.

_____

_____

_____

_____

ISBN: 9780170229838

c

Greener Gifts
Sales Journal   **Page 1**

		Inv no	Ref	Total $	Sales $	GST payable $	Cost of goods sold $

d

Greener Gifts
General Ledger

Accounts receivable	120

Inventory	130

GST payable	310

Sales	610

Cost of goods sold	710

ISBN: 9780170229838

 PHOTOCOPYING PROHIBITED   **Accounts Receivable Subsystem**

Sales Returns and Allowances

Sometimes goods may be returned by customers because they are damaged or faulty in some way, or they may not be what was ordered. On these occasions, the customer must be issued with a **credit note** for the goods returned. Credit notes may also be issued if customers have been accidentally overcharged, or if they agree to accept damaged goods for a cheaper price rather than return them.

The details shown on a credit note are almost exactly the same as those on an invoice. The requirements for GST purposes are also similar. The credit note normally has a space to record the original invoice number. This can be helpful in relating the two transactions and can prevent credit notes from being issued for goods which were bought from another supplier.

Suppose that *Handy Hardware* returned 500 of the whatsits that they had purchased from *Bitz 'n Pieces* The credit note is shown below.

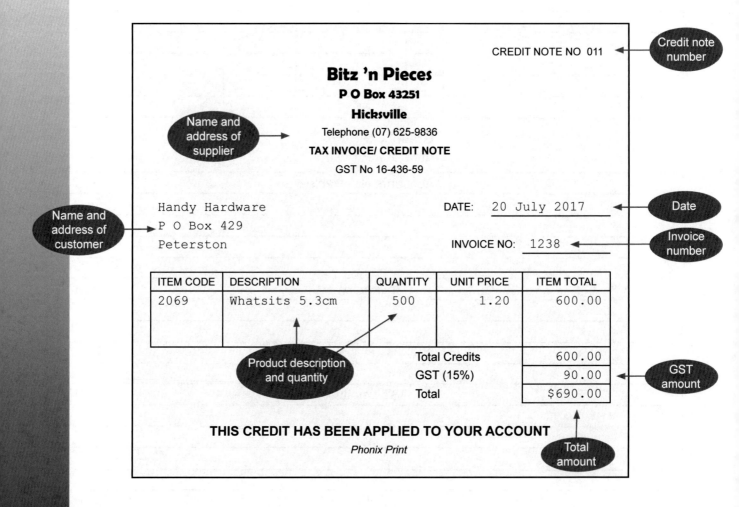

Control over Credit Notes

Tighter security is required over credit notes than for invoices. This is because a customer is unlikely to object to a credit, but will definitely object if an incorrect invoice is detected. All credit notes must be authorised by a senior member of staff. It is preferable that they are not issued by those staff issuing invoices.

Before issuing the credit note, the goods should be physically checked and it should be established that they were actually sold by the firm in the first instance. Staff responsible for updating debtors' records should not have access to credit note books. (Why?)

Consider the following example:
Kiri's Krafts issued the following credit notes in September 2019:

Date	Customer Name	Credit Note No	Selling price $	Cost price $
Sep 6	Rotorua Souvenirs	010	230	94
15	Te Anau Travel	011	69	—
20	Kerikeri Store	012	46	25

Note: The transaction on 15 September shows no entry in the cost of goods sold column. This is because it represents an allowance made to *Te Anau Travel*, rather than the physical return of goods.

The credit notes are recorded in the **sales returns and allowances** journal, which is another of the special journals, as follows:

Kiri's Krafts
Sales Returns and Allowances Journal Page 1

Date		Particulars	Credit Note No	Ref	Total $	Sales returns/ allow $	GST $	Cost of goods sold $
Sep	6	Rotorua Souvenirs	010		230	200	30	94
	15	Te Anau Travel	011		69	60	9	—
	20	Kerikeri Store	012		46	40	6	25
					$345	$300	$45	$119

Posting to the Ledger

Once again, we must record **two** aspects of the transaction when goods are returned:
- the total amount of the credit given to the customer
- the cost of goods that were returned.

If, as in the case of 15 September, no goods were returned, then only the total amount of the credit is recorded.

We represent the total credit on the accounting equation as follows:

Recording sales returns and allowances

	A	+	Ex	=	L	+	Eq	+	I
	Accounts receivable				**GST payable**				**Sales returns**
Credit notes issued $345	− 345			=	− 45				− 300
	Credit				**Debit**				**Debit**

Since the sales income has been reduced by the amount of the returns, we would make a *debit* entry to the income account. However, it is often useful for management decision-making to keep a separate record of the amount of returns received from customers. For example, an increase in the number of returns may indicate that the warehouse has become inefficient, that more goods are being damaged in transit, or that some new product lines are not of acceptable quality.

Thus, instead of posting the debit directly to the sales account, we create a new account, the **sales returns and allowances** account, to record these entries. This account is *contra* to the sales account and the balance is deducted from sales in the income statement.

> **Remember!**
>
> A *contra* account reduces the balance of another account in the ledger.

ISBN: 9780170229838

Accounts Receivable Subsystem

Ledger postings require the following entries:

Debit entries	$	Credit entries	$
GST payable	45	Accounts receivable	345
Sales returns and allowances	300		
	$345		$345

We must debit the GST account in this instance because the GST was recorded as a liability when the goods were first sold. Since the sale did not actually eventuate, the GST does not have to be paid and must be reversed.

The relevant accounts in the general ledger, after these entries have been posted, are shown in both formats, below and on the next page.

Kiri's Krafts
General Ledger

Accounts receivable — 120

Date	Particulars	Ref	$	Date	Particulars	Ref	$
Sep 1	Balance	b/d	6,900	Sep 30	Sales returns and allowances and GST	SRJ1	345
30	Sales and GST	SJ1	7,912				

GST payable — 310

Date	Particulars	Ref	$	Date	Particulars	Ref	$
Sep 30	Accounts receivable	SRJ1	45	Sep 1	Balance	b/d	1,200
				30	Accounts receivable	SJ1	1,032

Sales returns and allowances — 611

Date	Particulars	Ref	$	Date	Particulars	Ref	$
Sep 30	Accounts receivable	SRJ1	300				

Kiri's Krafts
General Ledger

Accounts receivable — 120

Date	Particulars	Ref	Dr $	Cr $	Balance $
Sep 1	Balance	b/d			6,900 Dr
30	Sales and GST	SJ1	7,912		14,812 Dr
	Sales returns and allowances and GST	SRJ1		345	14,467 Dr

GST payable — 310

Date	Particulars	Ref	Dr $	Cr $	Balance $
Sep 1	Balance	b/d			1,200 Cr
30	Accounts receivable	SJ1		1,032	2,232 Cr
	Accounts receivable	SRJ1	45		2,187 Cr

Sales returns and allowances — 611

Date	Particulars	Ref	Dr $	Cr $	Balance $
Sep 30	Accounts receivable	SRJ1	300		300 Dr

Important!

- The posting reference in the ledger accounts is 'SRJ1'. This stands for 'Sales Returns and Allowances Journal, Page 1'.

Recording inventory returned

$$A \quad + \quad Ex \quad = \quad L \quad + \quad Eq \quad + \quad I$$
Inventory   **Cost of goods sold**

Cost of inventory
returned, $119   − 119   + 119
              Debit   **Credit**

Ledger postings require the following entries:

Debit entries	$	Credit entries	$
Inventory	119	Cost of goods sold	119

NO GST!

GST was accounted for when the goods were originally purchased.

The relevant accounts in the general ledger, after these entries have been posted, appear as follows

Kiri's Krafts General Ledger

Inventory — 130

Date	Particulars	Ref	$	Date	Particulars	Ref	$
Sep 1	Balance	b/d	6,500	30	Cost of goods sold	SJ1	4,325
30	Cost of goods sold	SRJ1	119				

Cost of goods sold — 710

Date	Particulars	Ref	$	Date	Particulars	Ref	$
Sep 1	Balance	b/d	26,150	Sep 30	Inventory	SRJ1	119
30	Inventory	SJ1	4,325				

Kiri's Krafts General Ledger

Inventory — 130

Date	Particulars	Ref	Dr $	Cr $	Balance $
Sep 1	Balance	b/d			6,500 Dr
30	Cost of goods sold	SJ1		4,325	2,175 Dr
	Cost of goods sold	SRJ1	119		2,294 Dr

Cost of goods sold					710
Date	Particulars	Ref	Dr $	Cr $	Balance $
Sep 1	Balance	b/d			26,150 Dr
30	Inventory	SJ1	4,325		30,475 Dr
	Inventory	**SRJ1**		119	30,356 Dr

After posting has been completed, the sales returns and allowances journal appears as follows:

		Kiri's Krafts					
		Sales Returns and Allowances Journal					**Page 1**
Date		Particulars	Credit Note No	Ref	Total $	Sales returns/ allow $	GST $	Cost of goods sold $
Sep	6	Rotorua Souvenirs	010		230	200	30	94
	15	Te Anau Travel	011		69	60	9	—
	20	Kerikeri Store	012		46	40	6	25
					$345	$300	$45	$119
					120	611	310	130/710

Important!

- The posting reference for each column is shown below the total. In the cost of goods sold column, the reference (130/710) means that account 130 (inventory) is to be debited and account 710 (cost of goods sold) is to be credited.

- There is no entry in the cost of goods sold column for the transaction on 15 September because no physical goods were returned.

- The chart of accounts number for sales returns and allowances is 611. This follows immediately after the sales account 610, because it is a *contra* account.

- No entries are to be made in the reference column at this stage. This column is used for posting to individual debtor's accounts which we will do later.

Cash Receipts from Customers

Details of cash received from customers must also be posted to the accounts receivable account since cash payments reduce the amount owing to the firm. Cash paid by debtors is recorded in the **cash receipts** journal. When the invoice basis is used for GST, no GST is recorded when debtors pay their accounts, because it had already been done when the invoice was issued.

Sometimes, however, customers are given discounts on their accounts for prompt payment. In these cases, the amount of cash collected is less than the amount owing, resulting in an expense called **discount allowed**. In these cases, the GST account must be adjusted.

Note

Discounts allowed are for prompt payment of accounts. Sales discounts (reductions in the selling price) are *not* recorded in the journals.

 PHOTOCOPYING PROHIBITED

ISBN: 9780170229838

Calculating the GST on Discount Allowed

When an invoice is issued under the invoice basis for GST, the GST component is recorded as a liability on the date that the invoice is issued. Thus there is a liability for GST even though the cash has not been received from the customer.

Example:

An invoice is issued for $3,450. The ledger posting entries would be:

Debit entries	$	Credit entries	$
Accounts receivable	3,450	GST payable	450
		Sales	3,000
	$3,450		$3,450

Suppose that the customer pays his or her account on time and is given a 2% discount for prompt payment. The amount of the discount is thus:

$$\text{Discount} = 2\% \times \$3,450$$
$$= \$69$$
$$\text{Amount paid} = \$3,450 - 69$$
$$= \$3,381$$

The GST component of the amount that was collected from the customer is thus:

$$\text{GST component} = \frac{3}{23} \times \$3,381$$
$$= \$441$$

The business has already paid GST of **$450** to IRD, before collecting the cash from this customer. When the cash was received, only **$441** of GST was collected. This represents a shortfall of $450 – $441 = $9 of GST.

The total discount given to the customer was $69. However, as we have just seen, $9 of this amount represents GST that was not collected. This $9 is the GST component of the discount allowed:

$$\text{GST component} = \frac{3}{23} \times \$69$$
$$= \$9$$

The $9 overpaid GST will be claimed back from IRD in the next GST return. It thus represents a *reduction* in the GST payable account, requiring a **debit** entry.

Example (continued):

The customer owing $3,450 was given a 2% discount ($69) for prompt payment. This discount allowed included GST of $9. The ledger posting entries would be:

Debit entries	$	Credit entries	$
Discount allowed	60	Accounts receivable	69
GST payable	9		
	$69		$69

Let's return to *Kiri's Krafts*. The following is an extract from the cash receipts journal for September 2019, after the journal has been posted to the ledger:

Kiri's Krafts
Cash Receipts Journal (extract)

Date		Particulars	Receipt No	Ref	Discount allowed $	GST on discount $	Cash $	Accounts receivable $
Sep	15	Colinette's Crafts	232		—	—	230	230
	17	Te Anau Travel	234		—	—	1,840	1,840
	19	Rotorua Souvenirs	235		100	15	2,185	2,300
	20	Kerikeri Store	237		80	12	1,288	1,380
					$180	$27	[5,543]	$5,750
					730	310		120

Important!

Note

Normal business terms of trade require customers to pay their accounts by the 20th of the month following the issue of the invoice or statement.

- There are three new columns in this journal: discount allowed, GST on discount and accounts receivable.
- There is no total shown for the cash column because this is an extract only. In addition to accounts receivable, there would be other types of cash receipts in the full journal.
- The amount entered in the accounts receivable column is the total amount which will be credited to the debtor as a result of the transaction. This includes both the cash received and any discount which has been allowed to the debtor for prompt payment of his or her account. For example, on September 19, *Rotorua Souvenirs* paid $2,185 and was given a discount of $115. The amount credited to accounts receivable for this transaction will thus be $2,185 + 115 = $2,300.

Recording cash received and discount allowed

	A	+	Ex	=	L	+	Eq + I
	Cash	Accounts receivable	Discount allowed		GST payable		

Cash received from debtors, $5,543
discount allowed, $207   + 5,543   − 5,750   + 180   =   − 27

                Debit   **Credit**   **Debit**   **Debit**

Ledger postings require the following entries:

GST!

GST of $27 relating to discounts has been overpaid. This must be claimed from IRD later.

Debit entries	$	Credit entries	$
Cash	5,543	Accounts receivable	5,750
Discount allowed	180		
GST payable	27		
	$5,750		$5,750

PHOTOCOPYING PROHIBITED

ISBN: 9780170229852

The relevant accounts in the general ledger, after these entries have been posted, are shown in both formats below.

Kiri's Krafts General Ledger

Accounts receivable — 120

Date	Particulars	Ref	$	Date	Particulars	Ref	$
Sep 1	Balance	b/d	6,900	Sep 30	Sales returns and allowances and GST	SRJ1	345
30	Sales and GST	SJ1	7,912		Cash, discount allowed and GST	CRJ1	5,750

GST payable — 310

Date	Particulars	Ref	$	Date	Particulars	Ref	$
Sep 30	Accounts receivable	SRJ1	45	Sep 1	Balance	b/d	1,200
	Accounts receivable	CRJ1	27	30	Accounts receivable	SJ1	1,032

Discount allowed — 730

Date	Particulars	Ref	$	Date	Particulars	Ref	$
Sep 30	Accounts receivable	CRJ1	180				

Kiri's Krafts General Ledger

Accounts receivable — 120

Date	Particulars	Ref	Dr $	Cr $	Balance $
Sep 1	Balance	b/d			6,900 Dr
30	Sales and GST	SJ1	7,912		14,812 Dr
	Sales returns and allowances and GST	SRJ1		345	14,467 Dr
	Cash, discount allowed and GST	CRJ1		5,750	8,717 Dr

GST payable — 310

Date	Particulars	Ref	Dr $	Cr $	Balance $
Sep 1	Balance	b/d			1,200 Cr
30	Accounts receivable	SJ1		1,032	2,232 Cr
	Accounts receivable	SRJ1	45		2,187 Cr
	Accounts receivable	CRJ1	27		2,160 Cr

Discount allowed — 730

Date	Particulars	Ref	Dr $	Cr $	Balance $
Sep 30	Accounts receivable	CRJ1	180		180 Dr

ISBN: 9780170229852

Activities

1 One of the objectives of the accounts receivable subsystem is: *to ensure that credit notes are issued only for bona fide (genuine) returns* (see page 6). Explain how entering the original invoice number on the credit note assists in meeting this objective.

_____

_____

_____

_____

_____

_____

_____

2 Before issuing a credit note *when the wrong goods have been shipped*, it is normal procedure to physically inspect the goods that have been returned. Explain how this process helps to **safeguard the business assets**.

_____

_____

_____

_____

_____

_____

_____

3 Credit notes are sometimes issued without goods having been returned. Identify TWO examples of events that could give rise to this situation.

1. _____

_____

2. _____

_____

_____

4 Two of the internal controls relating to the issue of credit notes are *separation of duties* and *proper procedures for authorisation*.

a Explain the meaning of **separation of duties** and give an example in relation to the issue of credit notes.

_____

_____

_____

_____

_____

_____

Accounting – A Next Step   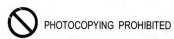   ISBN: 9780170229852

b Explain the meaning of **proper procedures for authorisation** and give an example in relation to the issue of credit notes.

_____

_____

_____

_____

_____

A common fraud in manual accounting systems was committed as follows:
- A customer paid his account to the cashier in cash
- The cashier pocketed the cash and issued a credit note to cover the loss
- The customer did not detect the fraud because the credit still showed on his statement.

c Explain how **separation of duties** could prevent the fraud taking place.

_____

_____

_____

_____

d Explain how **proper procedures for authorisation** could prevent the fraud taking place.

_____

_____

_____

_____

_____

5 One of the purposes of accounting is to provide information for management decision-making. When credit notes are issued, they are recorded in the sales returns and allowances journal and posted to a separate ledger account from sales. However, the same overall result would be achieved by posting sales returns and allowances directly to the debit side of the sales account in the general ledger.

DO THIS!

Fully explain how the use of a separate ledger account for sales returns and allowances assists management in the decision-making process.

_____

_____

_____

_____

_____

_____

_____

_____

_____

6 *Takapuna Trade* is registered for GST on the invoice basis. The following balances were extracted from the ledger at 1 July 2019:

Accounts receivable	$5,980 Dr	Sales	$19,000 Cr
Inventory	26,400 Dr	Sales returns and allowances	840 Dr
Cost of goods sold	8,500 Dr	GST payable	760 Cr
Discount allowed	1,120 Dr		

The documents below are from transactions with customers that occurred during the month of July.

TAX INVOICE No: 721 1 July 2019 **Takapuna Trade** INVOICE GST No: 41-568-95 TO: Andy's Decorating FOR: Ladder Total (incl GST) $460.00	TAX INVOICE No: 722 9 July 2019 **Takapuna Trade** INVOICE GST No: 41-568-95 TO: Pete's Painters FOR: Paint Total (incl GST) $345.00	TAX INVOICE No: 723 12 July 2019 **Takapuna Trade** INVOICE GST No: 41-568-95 TO: John's Jobs FOR: Scaffolding Total (incl GST) $2,875.00
TAX INVOICE No: 724 15 July 2019 **Takapuna Trade** INVOICE GST No: 41-568-95 TO: Kerry's Construction FOR: Sundry materials Total (incl GST) $115.00	TAX INVOICE No: 725 18 July 2019 **Takapuna Trade** INVOICE GST No: 41-568-95 TO: Sparky's FOR: Electric drill Total (incl GST) $230.00	TAX INVOICE No: 726 20 July 2019 **Takapuna Trade** INVOICE GST No: 41-568-95 TO: Pete's Painters FOR: Wallpaper Total (incl GST) $690.00
TAX INVOICE No: 727 20 July 2019 **Takapuna Trade** INVOICE GST No: 41-568-95 TO: Kerry's Construction FOR: Sundry materials Total (incl GST) $345.00	TAX INVOICE No: 728 26 July 2019 **Takapuna Trade** INVOICE GST No: 41-568-95 TO: Andy's Decorating FOR: Paint Total (incl GST) $920.00	TAX INVOICE No: 729 30 July 2019 **Takapuna Trade** INVOICE GST No: 41-568-95 TO: Pete's Painters FOR: Wallpaper Total (incl GST) $1,035.00
TAX INVOICE No: 109 Inv Ref: 727 22 July 2019 **Takapuna Trade** CREDIT NOTE GST No: 41-568-95 TO: Kerry's Construction FOR: Sundry materials Total (incl GST) $46.00	TAX INVOICE No: 110 Inv Ref: 725 26 July 2019 **Takapuna Trade** CREDIT NOTE GST No: 41-568-95 TO: Sparky's FOR: Electric drill Total (incl GST) $230.00	No: 946 18 July 2019 **Takapuna Trade** RECEIPT GST No: 41-568-95 TO: Kerry's Construction FOR: June account $828.00 (discount $92.00)
No: 947 19 July 2019 **Takapuna Trade** RECEIPT GST No: 41-568-95 FROM: Andy's Decorating FOR: June account Amount paid $1,449.00 (discount $161.00)	No: 948 20 July 2019 **Takapuna Trade** RECEIPT GST No: 41-568-95 FROM: Pete's Painters FOR: June account Amount paid $1,242.00 (discount $138.00)	No: 949 24 July 2019 **Takapuna Trade** RECEIPT GST No: 41-568-95 FROM: John's Jobs FOR: June account Amount paid $575.00

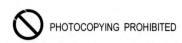

ISBN: 9780170229852

DO THIS!

a Prepare the July sales and sales returns and allowances journals for *Takapuna Trade*.
Note: The cost of goods sold is 50% of the GST exclusive selling price in every case.
b Complete the extract provided from the July cash receipts journal.
c Post the journals to the ledger accounts provided and balance all of the accounts except the GST payable account. (The chart of accounts references are given on the ledger accounts.)

a

Takapuna Trade
Sales Journal   **Page 9**

		Inv no	Ref	Total $	Sales $	GST payable $	Cost of goods sold $

Takapuna Trade
Sales Returns and Allowances Journal   **Page 2**

		C/N no	Ref	Total $	Sales returns & allowances $	GST payable $	Cost of goods sold $

ISBN: 9780170229852

b

Takapuna Trade
Cash Receipts Journal (extract)　　　　　　　　**Page 5**

		Rec no	Ref	Discount allowed $	GST on discount $	Cash $	Accounts receivable $

c　　　　　　　　　　　　　　　**Takapuna Trade**
General Ledger

Accounts receivable	120

Inventory	130

GST payable	310

Sales	610

Sales returns and allowances	611

Accounting – A Next Step　　　PHOTOCOPYING PROHIBITED　　ISBN: 9780170229852

Cost of goods sold	710

Discount allowed	720

7 The extracts below have been taken from the books of *Lighter Lamps* for the month of October 2018. The firm is registered for GST on the invoice basis.

Cash receipts journal (page 9) extract:

Particulars	Discount allowed	GST on discount	Cash	GST payable	Accounts receivable	Sales	Other receipts
TOTALS	900	135	30,475	2,310	13,800	14,400	1,000

		Cost of goods sold
Sales journal (page 7) invoice total:	$16,675	$11,280
Sales returns and allowances (page 3) journal credit note total:	989	650

Trial balance extract at 30 September 2018:

Accounts receivable	$14,950 Dr	Sales	$170,000 Cr
Inventory	36,700 Dr	Sales returns and allowances	8,200 Dr
Cost of goods sold	80,500 Dr	GST payable	1,760 Cr
Discount allowed	4,300 Dr	Cash	35,800 Dr

Lighter Lamps

DO THIS!

a Post the journals to the ledger accounts provided below and balance all of the accounts except the GST payable account.
b Explain to the business owner why an adjustment to GST payable is necessary when accounts receivable are given discounts for paying their accounts promptly.

a

Lighter Lamps
General Ledger

Accounts receivable	120

a

Inventory	130

GST payable	310

Sales	610

Sales returns and allowances	611

Cost of goods sold	710

Discount allowed	720

b Explain to the business owner why an adjustment to GST payable is necessary when accounts receivable are given discounts for paying their accounts promptly.

_____

_____

_____

_____

_____

_____

_____

Accounting – A Next Step

ISBN: 9780170229852

Sundry charges to debtors

Sometimes a firm charges its customers for additional items such as freight or cartage for delivery and interest or an overdue fee for non-payment of accounts. These charges are not sales of *goods*, and are not recorded in the *sales* journal.

Transactions that do not appear in the special journals (cash receipts, cash payments, sales, sales returns and allowances, purchases, purchases returns and allowances) appear in the **general journal** and are posted from there to the ledger.

Consider the following example:

During September, *Kiri's Krafts* made the following charges to customers:

- Freight of $69 (including GST) was charged to *Te Anau Travel* on 12 September, invoice 204.
- On 21 September, *Hikurangi House* was charged interest of $23. (**Note:** No GST is charged on interest.)

These transactions are recorded as follows:

Recording freight

	A	+	Ex	=	L	+	Eq	+	I
	Accounts receivable				**GST payable**				**Freight outwards**
Freight charged $69	+ 69			=	+ 9				+ 60
	Debit				**Credit**				**Credit**

Ledger postings require the following entries:

Debit entries	$	Credit entries	$
Accounts receivable	69	GST payable	9
		Freight outwards	60
	$69		**$69**

GST!

GST of $9 has been invoiced. This must be paid to IRD later.

In the accounting records, these entries are entered *first* in the general journal. The journal entry appears as follows:

	Kiri's Krafts General Journal			Page 1
Date	Particulars	Ref	Dr $	Cr $
Sep 12	Accounts receivable	120	69	
	GST payable	310		9
	Freight outwards	620		60
	(for freight charged to Te Anau Travel –			
	Invoice No 204)			

Note

Freight is often added to the sales invoice. In this case, it is recorded in a separate column in the *sales journal*, rather than in the general journal.

Recording interest

	A	+	Ex	=	L	+	Eq	+	I
	Accounts receivable								**Interest**
Interest charged $23	+ 23			=					+ 23
	Debit								**Credit**

NO GST!

Ledger postings require the following entries:

Debit entries	$	Credit entries	$
Accounts receivable	23	Interest	23
	$23		**$23**

No GST is charged on interest.

The general journal entry is:

<table>
<tr><td colspan="6" align="center">**Kiri's Krafts**
General Journal   **Page 1**</td></tr>
<tr><td>*Date*</td><td>*Particulars*</td><td>*Ref*</td><td>*Dr $*</td><td>*Cr $*</td></tr>
<tr><td>Sep 21</td><td>Accounts receivable</td><td>120</td><td>23</td><td></td></tr>
<tr><td></td><td> Interest</td><td>630</td><td></td><td>23</td></tr>
<tr><td></td><td>*(for interest charged to Hikurangi*
House)</td><td></td><td></td><td></td></tr>
</table>

Important!

- The page number of the general journal is shown at the top of the page.
- The *debit* entry or entries are recorded first, followed by the *credit* entry or entries.
- In the *Particulars* column, the credit entry is slightly indented.
- Each account has its reference number from the chart of accounts in the reference column. This is called a **posting reference**. It enables us to trace the ledger account where the entry will be posted.
- At the bottom of each entry there is a sentence in brackets which explains the transaction. This sentence is called a **narration**.

The relevant accounts in the general ledger, after these entries have been posted, are shown in both formats below and on the next page.

Kiri's Krafts
General Ledger

Accounts receivable   **120**

Date	Particulars	Ref	$	Date	Particulars	Ref	$
Sep 1	Balance	b/d	6,900	Sep 30	Sales returns		
12	**Freight outwards**				and allowances		
	and GST	GJ1	69		and GST	SRJ1	345
21	**Interest**	GJ1	23		Cash, discount		
30	Sales and GST	SJ1	7,912		allowed and GST	CRJ1	5,750

GST payable   **310**

Date	Particulars	Ref	$	Date	Particulars	Ref	$
Sep 30	Accounts			Sep 1	Balance	b/d	1,200
	receivable	SRJ1	45	12	**Accounts**	GJ1	9
	Accounts				**receivable**		
	receivable	CRJ1	27	30	Accounts		
					receivable	SJ1	1,032

Freight outwards   **620**

Date	Particulars	Ref	$	Date	Particulars	Ref	$
				Sep 12	**Accounts**		
					receivable	GJ1	60

Interest   **630**

Date	Particulars	Ref	$	Date	Particulars	Ref	$
				Sep 21	**Accounts**		
					receivable	GJ1	23

Important!

- Postings from the general journal are carried out *daily*. This means that the dates of the individual transactions appear in the ledger accounts.

Kiri's Krafts
General Ledger

Accounts receivable   120

Date	Particulars	Ref	Dr $	Cr $	Balance $
Sep 1	Balance	b/d			6,900 Dr
12	**Freight outwards and GST**	**GJ1**	**69**		6,969 Dr
21	**Interest**	**GJ1**	**23**		6,992 Dr
30	Sales and GST	SJ1	7,912		14,904 Dr
	Sales returns and allowances and GST	SRJ1		345	14,559 Dr
	Cash, discount allowed and GST	CRJ1		5,750	8,809 Dr

GST payable   310

Date	Particulars	Ref	Dr $	Cr $	Balance $
Sep 1	Balance	b/d			1,200 Cr
12	**Accounts receivable**	**GJ1**		9	1,209 Cr
30	Accounts receivable	SJ1		1,032	2,241 Cr
	Accounts receivable	SRJ1	45		2,196 Cr
	Accounts receivable	CRJ1	27		2,169 Cr

Freight outwards   620

Date	Particulars	Ref	Dr $	Cr $	Balance $
Sep 12	**Accounts receivable**	**GJ1**		60	60 Cr

Interest   630

Date	Particulars	Ref	Dr $	Cr $	Balance $
Sep 21	**Accounts receivable**	**GJ1**		23	23 Cr

Note

The general journal entries for freight and interest are posted daily. They have been inserted into the ledger here in date order. The running balances therefore differ from previous accounts in this example.

Collecting your Accounts

The continued operation of the business depends upon the fast collection of accounts receivable because:

- Cash tied up in accounts receivable is not available for other purposes such as paying creditors, drawings, or buying property, plant and equipment.
- If the firm has a bank overdraft, interest on this can quickly erode the profit margin of a sale.
- Surplus cash can be invested to earn a return if debtors pay on time.
- The more time you let your debtors have to pay, very often the less chance you have of collecting your money.

Remember!

Before you sell on credit:
- Have a credit policy laid down
- Make sure your customers are aware of it.

 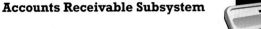

Even if the credit policy is firmly established, there are many reasons that bad debts may still arise. Some of these are:

- an economic downturn
- seasonal fluctuations, e.g. agricultural industries
- the customers may have poor credit control themselves, thus not be collecting cash owing to them.

There are some precautions which can be taken to help minimise bad debts:

- Send regular statements to customers
- Offer discounts for prompt payment
- Charge interest on overdue accounts
- Mark accounts 'OVERDUE' with a coloured label to attract attention
- Make personal contact through email, letter or (preferably) telephone call
- Make personal visits
- Use debt collection agencies as a last resort for sizeable debts. (Debt collectors charge fees and/or commission so may not be worthwhile for small debts.)

A debt should be declared bad only if all reasonable action has been taken to recover it, or if the customer has been declared bankrupt.

Consider the following example:

Russell Store owes $690 to *Kiri's Krafts*. Unfortunately the owner became ill and the store was forced to close, being unable to pay its debts. *Kiri's Krafts* wrote the total amount owing off as a bad debt on 30 September.

Recording bad debts

	A + Accounts receivable	Ex = Bad debts	L + GST payable	Eq + I
Bad debt written off, $690	– 690	+ 600 =	– 90	
	Credit	Debit	Debit	

Ledger postings require the following entries:

Debit entries	$	Credit entries	$
Bad debts	600	Accounts receivable	690
GST payable	90		
	$690		$690

GST of $90 relating to bad debts has already been paid. This must be claimed from IRD later.

Bad debts are recorded in the **general journal**.

Note

Sometimes a partial settlement may be received from a bankrupt customer. In this case only that portion of the account which has not been recovered is written off.

Kiri's Krafts
General Journal Page 1

Date	Particulars	Ref	Dr $	Cr $
Sep 30	Bad debts	740	600	
	GST payable	310	90	
	Accounts receivable	120		690
	(for Russell Store account written off)			

The relevant accounts in the general ledger, after these entries have been posted, are shown in both formats on the next page.

 PHOTOCOPYING PROHIBITED

ISBN: 9780170229852

Kiri's Krafts – General Ledger

Accounts receivable — 120

Date	Particulars	Ref	$	Date	Particulars	Ref	$
Sep 1	Balance	b/d	6,900	Sep 30	Sales returns and allowances and GST	SRJ1	345
12	Freight outwards and GST	GJ1	69		Cash, discount allowed and GST	CRJ1	5,750
21	Interest	GJ1	23		**Bad debts and GST**	**GJ1**	**690**
30	Sales and GST	SJ1	7,912		Balance	c/f	8,119
			$14,904				$14,904
Oct 1	Balance	b/d	8,119				

GST payable — 310

Date	Particulars	Ref	$	Date	Particulars	Ref	$
Sep 30	Accounts receivable	SRJ1	45	Sep 1	Balance	b/d	1,200
	Accounts receivable	CRJ1	27	12	Accounts receivable	GJ1	9
	Accounts receivable	**GJ1**	**90**	30	Accounts receivable	SJ1	1,032

Bad debts — 740

Date	Particulars	Ref	$	Date	Particulars	Ref	$
Sep 30	**Accounts receivable**	**GJ1**	**600**				

Kiri's Krafts – General Ledger

Accounts receivable — 120

Date	Particulars	Ref	Dr $	Cr $	Balance $
Sep 1	Balance	b/d			6,900 Dr
12	Freight outwards and GST	GJ1	69		6,969 Dr
21	Interest	GJ1	23		6,992 Dr
30	Sales and GST	SJ1	7,912		14,904 Dr
	Sales returns and allowances and GST	SRJ1		345	14,559 Dr
	Cash, discount allowed and GST	CRJ1		5,750	8,809 Dr
	Bad debts and GST	**GJ1**		**690**	8,119 Dr

GST payable — 310

Date	Particulars	Ref	Dr $	Cr $	Balance $
Sep 1	Balance	b/d			1,200 Cr
12	Accounts receivable	GJ1		9	1,209 Cr
30	Accounts receivable	SJ1		1,032	2,241 Cr
	Accounts receivable	SRJ1	45		2,196 Cr
	Accounts receivable	CRJ1	27		2,169 Cr
	Accounts receivable	**GJ1**	**90**		2,079 Cr

Bad debts — 740

Date	Particulars	Ref	Dr $	Cr $	Balance $
Sep 12	**Accounts receivable**	**GJ1**	**600**		600 Dr

ISBN: 9780170229852

1 Fully explain why entries to record the credit sale of property, plant and equipment do not appear in the **sales journal**.

_____

_____

_____

_____

_____

2 The following information has been extracted from the accounting records of *Fiona's Fashion Warehouse*. The firm is registered for GST on the invoice basis.

		Source
Accounts receivable balance, 1 May	$71,785	General ledger
Total invoices issued for goods during May	85,560	Sales journal, page 6
Total credit notes issued during May	4,600	Sales returns and allowances journal, page 2
Cash received from customers during May	69,230	Cash receipts journal, page 8
Discounts allowed to customers during May	1,806	Cash receipts journal, page 8

Additional information
- On 17 May, an invoice for cartage of $23 was sent to *Smart Gear*.
- On 23 May, interest of $92 was charged to *Best Dressed* for non-payment of April's account.
- On 31 May, the account of *Modern Madam*, amounting to $1,840 was written off as a bad debt.

DO THIS!

a Prepare general journal entries to record the transactions listed under *Additional Information* above.
b Prepare the accounts receivable account as it would appear in the ledger after balancing on 31 May.

a

Fiona's Fashion Warehouse
General Journal **Page 2**

Date	Particulars	Ref	Dr $	Cr $

b

Fiona's Fashion Warehouse
General Ledger

Accounts receivable	120

3 The extracts below have been taken from the books of *Heirloom Furniture* for the month of June 2020. The firm is registered for GST on the invoice basis.

Cash receipts journal (page 7) extract:

Particulars	Discount allowed	GST on discount	Cash	GST payable	Accounts receivable	Other receipts
TOTALS	2,200	330	54,395	495	50,600	5,830

		Cost of goods sold
Sales journal (page 5) invoice total:	$43,700	$18,500
Sales returns and allowances (page 2) journal credit note total:	1,035	420

HEIRLOOM
Bringing the past to life

General Journal — Page 2

Date	Particulars	Dr $	Cr $
Jun 11	Accounts receivable	3,220	
	GST payable		420
	Freight outwards		2,800
	(for freight charged to Antiques 4 All)		
25	Accounts receivable	230	
	Interest		230
	(for interest on overdue account charged to Bedroom Specialists)		
30	Bad debts	3,000	
	GST payable	450	
	Accounts receivable		3,450
	(to write off Elegant Homes' account)		

Trial balance extract at 30 June 2020:

Accounts receivable	$ 55,200 Dr	Sales	$80,000 Cr
Inventory	120,000 Dr	Sales returns and allowances	2,500 Dr
Cost of goods sold	36,000 Dr	GST payable	9,200 Cr
Discount allowed	6,325 Dr	Bad debts	4,100 Dr
Freight outwards	5,175 Cr	Interest charged	1,380 Cr

DO THIS!

Post the journals to the ledger accounts provided on the next page and balance the accounts. (The chart of accounts references are given on the ledger accounts.)

Heirloom Furniture
General Ledger

Accounts receivable			120

Inventory			130

Sales			610

Freight outwards			620

Interest			630

Sales returns and allowances			611

Cost of goods sold			710

Discount allowed			720

Bad debts			730

PHOTOCOPYING PROHIBITED

ISBN: 9780170229852

Accounts Receivable Subsidiary Ledger

Until now, all credit sales and sales returns have been recorded in the accounts receivable account in the ledger. This means that we have information about the total amount which is owed to the business by debtors.

While it is essential to have the total of accounts receivable in the statement of financial position, the total itself does not give managers the essential information they need to run the business on a day-to-day basis. To achieve efficient credit control, managers need to know who the business debtors are and how much each owes. Records of individual debtors are kept in a **subsidiary ledger**. This is a *separate* ledger which is outside the general ledger of the business.

A subsidiary ledger expands the information contained in a single account in the general ledger, called a **control account**. For example, an accounts receivable subsidiary ledger contains separate accounts for each individual debtor and the general ledger account is called the accounts receivable **control** account. Each transaction relating to a single debtor is recorded in a subsidiary ledger account and the totals are recorded in the accounts receivable control account as we have done throughout the chapter.

Let's return to *Kiri's Krafts*. The accounts receivable (control) account for September appeared as follows:

Kiri's Krafts – General Ledger

Accounts receivable control — 120

Date	Particulars	Ref	$	Date	Particulars	Ref	$
Sep 1	Balance	b/d	6,900	Sep 30	Sales returns and allowances and GST	SRJ1	345
12	Freight outwards and GST	GJ1	69		Cash, discount allowed and GST	CRJ1	5,750
21	Interest	GJ1	23		Bad debts and GST	GJ1	690
30	Sales and GST	SJ1	7,912		Balance	c/f	8,119
			$14,904				$14,904
Oct 1	Balance	b/d	8,119				

If we examine this account carefully, we can see that entries were posted from the following journals:

- General journal
- Cash receipts journal
- Sales journal
- Sales returns and allowances journal.

We are now about to create a new ledger, the **accounts receivable ledger**. This ledger will contain separate accounts for each of the debtors of *Kiri's Krafts*. Before we can begin, we must establish the opening balance of each of the individual debtors of the business. We prepare a **schedule of accounts receivable** at the end of August as follows:

Kiri's Krafts	
Schedule of Accounts Receivable as at 31 August 2018	
Kerikeri Store	$1,380
Rotorua Souvenirs	2,300
Te Anau Travel	1,840
Hikurangi House	460
Russell Store	690
Colinette's Crafts	230
Balance as per Control Account	$6,900

When the opening balances given in the schedule of accounts receivable have been entered in the accounts receivable ledger, the ledger appears as follows:

Kiri's Krafts
Accounts Receivable Ledger

Kerikeri Store — ARL1

Date	Particulars	Ref	$	Date	Particulars	Ref	$
Sep 1	Balance	b/d	1,380				

Rotorua Souvenirs — ARL2

Date	Particulars	Ref	$	Date	Particulars	Ref	$
Sep 1	Balance	b/d	2,300				

Te Anau Travel — ARL3

Date	Particulars	Ref	$	Date	Particulars	Ref	$
Sep 1	Balance	b/d	1,840				

Hikurangi House — ARL4

Date	Particulars	Ref	$	Date	Particulars	Ref	$
Sep 1	Balance	b/d	460				

Russell Store — ARL5

Date	Particulars	Ref	$	Date	Particulars	Ref	$
Sep 1	Balance	b/d	690				

Colinette's Crafts — ARL6

Date	Particulars	Ref	$	Date	Particulars	Ref	$
Sep 1	Balance	b/d	230				

Important!

- The accounts receivable ledger accounts are also numbered according to a chart of accounts. In this case we have simplified the account numbers, referring to them as ARL1 to ARL6. Different businesses will use different means of numbering subsidiary ledger accounts.
- The accounts receivable account is now called the accounts receivable **control** account. The use of the word *control* in an account name in the general ledger means that there is a subsidiary ledger attached to that account.
- The sum of the balances in the accounts receivable ledger equals the balance in the accounts receivable control account in the general ledger.
- The balances from the accounts receivable ledger do not appear in the trial balance. The trial balance contains only general ledger account balances. If we included the accounts from the subsidiary ledger, the balances would be included twice and the trial balance would not balance.

ISBN: 9780170229852

We can represent the relationship between the accounts receivable ledger and the accounts receivable control account in the general ledger in a diagram:

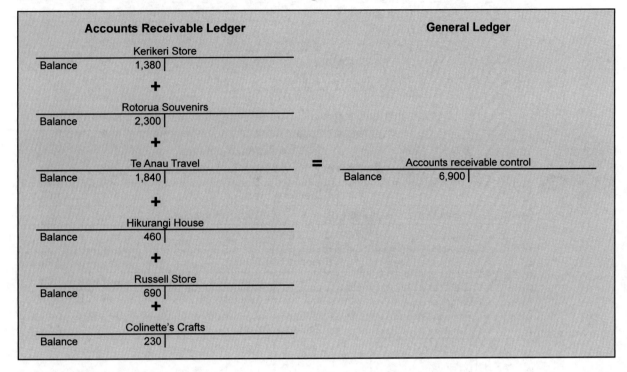

Posting the General Journal

When we posted the general journal to the accounts receivable control account in the previous section, we posted the journal entries on a *daily* basis. This was different from the posting of the special journals which was normally carried out on a *monthly* basis, on the last day of the month.

Posting of **all** journal entries to the subsidiary ledger is carried out on a *daily* basis. This is because the data from the subsidiary ledger accounts forms the basis of the monthly **statement** that is sent to the customer.

Now that we are using a subsidiary ledger as well as the general ledger, all entries which are posted to the accounts receivable control account must also be posted to the individual debtors' accounts in the accounts receivable ledger.

Since we are now posting the journal to two different ledgers, we need **two** posting references in the reference column of the journal. In the previous section there were transactions relating to *Te Anau Travel* (ARL3), *Hikurangi House* (ARL4) and *Russell Store* (ARL5). When these posting references have been added to the general journal, it appears as follows:

	Kiri's Krafts General Journal			Page 1
Date	Particulars	Ref	Dr $	Cr $
Sep 12	Accounts receivable – **Te Anau Travel**	120/ARL3	69	
	GST payable	310		9
	Freight outwards	620		60
	(for freight charged to Te Anau Travel – Invoice No 204)			
21	Accounts receivable – **Hikurangi House**	120/ARL4	23	
	Interest	630		23
	(for interest charged to Hikurangi House)			

Kiri's Krafts General Journal				Page 1
Date	Particulars	Ref	Dr $	Cr $
Sep 30	Bad debts	740	600	
	GST payable	310	90	
	Accounts receivable – **Russell Store**	**120/ARL5**		690
	(for Russell Store account written off)			

The accounts receivable ledger after these entries have been posted is:

Kiri's Krafts
Accounts Receivable Ledger

Kerikeri Store — ARL1

Date	Particulars	Ref	$	Date	Particulars	Ref	$
Sep 1	Balance	b/d	1,380				

Rotorua Souvenirs — ARL2

Date	Particulars	Ref	$	Date	Particulars	Ref	$
Sep 1	Balance	b/d	2,300				

Te Anau Travel — ARL3

Date	Particulars	Ref	$	Date	Particulars	Ref	$
Sep 1	Balance	b/d	1,840				
12	Freight outwards and GST	GJ1	69				

Hikurangi House — ARL4

Date	Particulars	Ref	$	Date	Particulars	Ref	$
Sep 1	Balance	b/d	460				
21	Interest	GJ1	23				

Russell Store — ARL5

Date	Particulars	Ref	$	Date	Particulars	Ref	$
Sep 1	Balance	b/d	690	Sep 30	Bad debts and GST	GJ1	690

Colinette's Crafts — ARL6

Date	Particulars	Ref	$	Date	Particulars	Ref	$
Sep 1	Balance	b/d	230				

Posting the Special Journals

Earlier in the chapter we prepared the sales journal and the sales returns and allowances journal. We then posted these, together with the relevant entries from the cash receipts journal, to the accounts receivable control account and other relevant general ledger accounts. When we posted these journals to the general ledger, we did not use their reference columns. Reference columns are used for the numbers from the chart of accounts from the accounts receivable ledger.

The journals are shown on the next page, after they have been posted to the subsidiary ledger. Note the use of the accounts receivable ledger account codes in the reference columns. Posting to the subsidiary ledger is carried out *daily*.

The T form accounts receivable control account is shown opposite and the 3-column form is on page 48. The accounts receivable ledger, after posting the journals, is shown in T form on page 46 and in 3-column form on page 47.

> **Important!**
>
> Entries to the subsidiary ledger accounts are posted *daily*. This is because the accounts form the basis of the customer statements.

Kiri's Krafts
Sales Journal
Page 1

Date		Particulars	Invoice No	Ref	Total $	Sales $	GST $	Cost of goods sold $
Sep	1	Rotorua Souvenirs	201	ARL2	2,300	2,000	300	940
	8	Kerikeri Store	202	ARL1	1,725	1,500	225	1,080
	12	Te Anau Travel	203	ARL3	1,150	1,000	150	645
	14	Hikurangi House	205	ARL4	276	240	36	120
	16	Kerikeri Store	206	ARL1	184	160	24	95
	20	Rotorua Souvenirs	207	ARL2	92	80	12	40
	22	Colinette's Crafts	208	ARL6	1,840	1,600	240	1,225
	25	Te Anau Travel	209	ARL3	345	300	45	180
					$7,912	$6,880	$1,032	$4,325
					120	610	310	710/130

Sales Returns and Allowances Journal
Page 1

Date		Particulars	Credit Note No	Ref	Total $	Sales returns/ allow $	GST $	Cost of goods sold $
Sep	6	Rotorua Souvenirs	010	ARL2	230	200	30	94
	15	Te Anau Travel	011	ARL3	69	60	9	—
	20	Kerikeri Store	012	ARL1	46	40	6	25
					$345	$300	$45	$119
					120	611	310	130/710

Cash Receipts Journal (extract)

Date		Particulars	Receipt No	Ref	Discount allowed $	GST on discount $	Cash $	Accounts receivable $
Sep	15	Colinette's Crafts	232	ARL6	—	—	230	230
	17	Te Anau Travel	234	ARL3	—	—	1,840	1,840
	19	Rotorua Souvenirs	235	ARL2	100	15	2,185	2,300
	20	Kerikeri Store	237	ARL1	80	12	1,288	1,380
					$180	$27	[5,543]	$5,750
					730	310		120

Kiri's Krafts – General Ledger

Accounts receivable control
120

Date	Particulars	Ref	$	Date	Particulars	Ref	$
Sep 1	Balance	b/d	6,900	Sep 30	Sales returns and allowances and GST	SRJ1	345
12	Freight outwards and GST	GJ1	69		Cash, discount allowed and GST	CRJ1	5,750
21	Interest	GJ1	23		Bad debts and GST	GJ1	690
30	Sales and GST	SJ1	7,912		Balance	c/f	8,119
			$14,904				$14,904
Oct 1	Balance	b/d	8,119				

Kiri's Krafts
Accounts Receivable Ledger

Kerikeri Store — ARL1

Date	Particulars	Ref	$	Date	Particulars	Ref	$
Sep 1	Balance	b/d	1,380	Sep 20	Sales returns and		
8	Sales and GST	SJ1	1,725		allowances and GST	SRJ1	46
16	Sales and GST	SJ1	184		Cash, discount		
					allowed and GST	CRJ1	1,380
				30	Balance	c/f	1,863
			$3,289				$3,289
Oct 1	Balance	b/d	1,863				

Rotorua Souvenirs — ARL2

Date	Particulars	Ref	$	Date	Particulars	Ref	$
Sep 1	Balance	b/d	2,300	Sep 6	Sales returns and		
	Sales and GST	SJ1	2,300		allowances and GST	SRJ1	230
20	Sales and GST	SJ1	92	19	Cash, discount		
					allowed and GST	CRJ1	2,300
				30	Balance	c/f	2,162
			$4,692				$4,692
Oct 1	Balance	b/d	2,162				

Te Anau Travel — ARL3

Date	Particulars	Ref	$	Date	Particulars	Ref	$
Sep 1	Balance	b/d	1,840	Sep 15	Sales returns and		
12	Freight outwards				allowances and GST	SRJ1	69
	and GST	GJ1	69	17	Cash	CRJ1	1,840
	Sales and GST	SJ1	1,150	30	Balance	c/f	1,495
25	Sales and GST	SJ1	345				
			$3,404				$3,404
Oct 1	Balance	b/d	1,495				

Hikurangi House — ARL4

Date	Particulars	Ref	$	Date	Particulars	Ref	$
Sep 1	Balance	b/d	460	Sep 30	Balance	c/f	759
14	Sales and GST	SJ1	276				
21	Interest	GJ1	23				
			$759				$759
Oct 1	Balance	b/d	759				

Russell Store — ARL5

Date	Particulars	Ref	$	Date	Particulars	Ref	$
Sep 1	Balance	b/d	690	Sep 30	Bad debts and GST	GJ1	690

Colinette's Crafts — ARL6

Date	Particulars	Ref	$	Date	Particulars	Ref	$
Sep 1	Balance	b/d	230	Sep 15	Cash	CRJ1	230
22	Sales and GST	SJ1	1,840	30	Balance	c/f	1,840
			$2,070				$2,070
Oct 1	Balance	b/d	1,840				

Accounting – A Next Step

PHOTOCOPYING PROHIBITED

ISBN: 9780170229852

Kiri's Krafts
Accounts Receivable Ledger

Kerikeri Store — ARL1

Date	Particulars	Ref	Dr $	Cr $	Balance $
Sep 1	Balance	b/d			1,380 Dr
8	Sales and GST	SJ1	1,725		3,105 Dr
16	Sales and GST	SJ1	184		3,289 Dr
20	Sales returns and allowances and GST	SRJ1		46	3,243 Dr
	Cash, discount allowed and GST	CRJ1		1,380	1,863 Dr

Rotorua Souvenirs — ARL2

Date	Particulars	Ref	Dr $	Cr $	Balance $
Sep 1	Balance	b/d			2,300 Dr
	Sales and GST	SJ1	2,300		4,600 Dr
6	Sales returns and allowances and GST	SRJ1		230	4,370 Dr
19	Cash, discount allowed and GST	CRJ1		2,300	2,070 Dr
20	Sales and GST	SJ1	92		2,162 Dr

Te Anau Travel — ARL3

Date	Particulars	Ref	Dr $	Cr $	Balance $
Sep 1	Balance	b/d			1,840 Dr
12	Freight outwards and GST	GJ1	69		1,909 Dr
	Sales and GST	SJ1	1,150		3,059 Dr
15	Sales returns and allowances and GST	SRJ1		69	2,990 Dr
17	Cash	CRJ1		1,840	1,150 Dr
25	Sales and GST	SJ1	345		1,495 Dr

Hikurangi House — ARL4

Date	Particulars	Ref	Dr $	Cr $	Balance $
Sep 1	Balance	b/d			460 Dr
14	Sales and GST	SJ1	276		736 Dr
21	Interest	GJ1	23		759 Dr

Russell Store — ARL5

Date	Particulars	Ref	Dr $	Cr $	Balance $
Sep 1	Balance	b/d			690 Dr
30	Bad debts and GST	GJ1		690	—

Colinette's Crafts — ARL6

Date	Particulars	Ref	Dr $	Cr $	Balance $
Sep 1	Balance	b/d			230 Dr
15	Cash	CRJ1		230	—
22	Sales and GST	SJ1	1,840		1,840 Dr

Remember!

The sum of the balances in the **accounts receivable *ledger*** equals the balance of the **accounts receivable *control account*** at the end of the month.

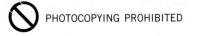  **Accounts Receivable Subsystem**

47

Kiri's Krafts – General Ledger

Accounts receivable control   **120**

Date	Particulars	Ref	Dr $	Cr $	Balance $
Sep 1	Balance	b/d			6,900 Dr
12	Freight outwards and GST	GJ1	69		6,969 Dr
21	Interest	GJ1	23		6,992 Dr
30	Sales and GST	SJ1	7,912		14,904 Dr
	Sales returns and allowances and GST	SRJ1		345	14,559 Dr
	Cash, discount allowed and GST	CRJ1		5,750	8,809 Dr
	Bad debts and GST	GJ1		690	8,119 Dr

The schedule of accounts receivable at the end of September is:

Kiri's Krafts
Schedule of Accounts Receivable as at 30 September 2018

Kerikeri Store	$1,863
Rotorua Souvenirs	2,162
Te Anau Travel	1,495
Hikurangi House	759
Colinette's Crafts	1,840
Balance as per Control Account	$8,119

The fact that the total of the individual accounts balances with the control account 'proves' the ledger. This is a useful form of control since the posting of the general and accounts receivable ledgers will often be done by different people.

Subsidiary ledgers are often called *self-balancing ledgers* because they must reconcile to a control account in the general ledger. In a purely manual system, the individual debtors' records were often kept on a set of cards. This enabled the work to be spread among a number of people. In a computerised system, both subsidiary ledger and control account balances are derived from the sales subsystem and internal checks exist to ensure that the balances reconcile.

Correction of errors

Reconciliation of the balances of the individual accounts with the control account does not detect posting errors where transactions have been posted to the wrong customer's account. The balance of the accounts receivable control account is not affected; neither is the total of the schedule of accounts receivable.

Often such errors are detected only when a customer complains. Thus the firm makes use of the customer as an extra check on the accuracy of its accounting records. These errors are corrected through an entry in the general journal.

Suppose that *Rotorua Souvenirs* notified *Kiri's Krafts* on 7 October that invoice 207 had been charged incorrectly to their account. Investigations found that this should have been charged to *Hikurangi House*. The general journal entry is:

Kiri's Krafts
General Journal   **Page 1**

Date	Particulars	Ref	Dr $	Cr $
Oct 7	Accounts receivable – **Hikurangi House**	ARL4	92	
	Accounts receivable – **Rotorua Souvenirs**	ARL2		92
	(to correct error in invoice 207 charged to Rotorua Souvenirs)			

Kiri's Krafts
Accounts Receivable Ledger

Rotorua Souvenirs ARL2

Date	Particulars	Ref	$	Date	Particulars	Ref	$
Oct 1	Balance	b/d	2,162	Oct 7	Accounts receivable – Hikurangi House	GJ1	92

Hikurangi House ARL4

Date	Particulars	Ref	$	Date	Particulars	Ref	$
Oct 1	Balance	b/d	759				
7	Accounts receivable – Rotorua Souvenirs	GJ1	92				

Advantages of Using Subsidiary Ledgers

- Excess detail is omitted from the general ledger by using a control account compared with holding a single account for every single debtor.

- A check for errors can be carried out through reconciling the balance of the control account with the total of the individual debtors' accounts.

- It is not necessary to prepare a complete trial balance to check the accuracy of the debtors' accounts. This would be necessary if the individual accounts were kept in the general ledger.

- Subdivision of the ledger into groups of customers can reinforce internal control through the rotation of duties among accounts receivable clerks.

Ageing of Accounts Receivable

Ageing of accounts means dividing the accounts receivable into groups, depending on how long they have been outstanding. An aged accounts receivable report can be prepared to show this information.

Consider the following example:

A firm has accounts receivable of $30,300. These have been broken down according to age and the following schedule prepared:

Aged Accounts Receivable Report as at 31 March 2020

Age of account	Debtor A	Debtor B	Debtor C	Total
Current	$13,000	$7,000		$20,000
1 month		1,800	700	2,500
2 months		1,600	2,000	3,600
3 months			2,400	2,400
Over 3 months			1,800	1,800
Total accounts receivable	$13,000	$10,400	$6,900	$30,300

The age of accounts receivable can provide a good indication of whether the debt will ever be repaid or not. The older the debt, the less likely it is to be collected. Debtor C above is in serious danger of becoming uncollectible. Debtor B should be followed up immediately and not receive any further credit.

A business *must* monitor the age of its debtors. This provides information that management can use to:

- monitor the efficiency of credit control and review credit control policies; and
- estimate future levels of bad debts.

Activities

(1) The extracts below are from the accounting records of *Anchors Aweigh* for the month of October 2021. The firm is registered for GST on the invoice basis.

Schedule of Accounts Receivable at 1 October

S Aylor	$460
S Knotts	345
B Oatee	920
F Isherman	550
R Admiral	1,150
	$3,425

Invoices Issued

Date	No		Amount
Oct 5	109	B Oatee	$207
8	110	F Isherman	92
11	111	R Admiral	345
14	112	S Aylor	322
20	113	B Oatee	483
24	114	N Ovice	161
28	115	S Aylor	69
			$1,679

Credit Notes Issued

Date	No		Amount
Oct 10	04	B Oatee	$ 92
20	05	S Aylor	115
31	06	N Ovice	23
			$230

Receipt Book

Date	Rec No		Cash	Discount allowed (inc GST)
Oct 7	217	B Oatee	$ 874	$46
12	218	S Aylor	437	23
22	219	R Admiral	1,150	—

General Journal

Date	Particulars	Dr $	Cr $
Oct 21	Accounts receivable – F Isherman	11	
	Interest		11
	(for interest charged to F Isherman)		
31	Bad debts	300	
	GST payable	45	
	Accounts receivable – S Knotts		345
	(to write off S Knotts' account)		

DO THIS!

a Prepare the accounts receivable control account and subsidiary ledger for October 2021. Posting references are **not** required.
b Prepare a schedule of accounts receivable.

a
Anchors Aweigh
General Ledger

Accounts receivable control	120

ISBN: 9780170229852

Anchors Aweigh
Accounts Receivable Ledger

S Aylor	ARL1

S Knotts	ARL2

B Oatee	ARL3

F Isherman	ARL4

R Admiral	ARL5

ISBN: 9780170229852

Accounts Receivable Subsystem

a

Anchors Aweigh
Accounts Receivable Ledger

N Ovice		ARL6

b

Anchors Aweigh
Schedule of Accounts Receivable as at 31 October 2021

DO THIS!

Answer the questions **c**, **d** and **e** below.

c S Aylor returned some goods on 12 October because he had ordered too many, and was issued with a credit note. List the steps that should have been taken in issuing this credit note. You should explain why each step is necessary.

_____
_____
_____
_____
_____
_____
_____

d Explain why R Admiral did not receive any discount when he paid his account.

_____
_____
_____
_____

e Explain the meaning of the general journal entry on 21 October and describe the situation that is most likely to have given rise to this entry.

_____
_____
_____
_____
_____

ISBN: 9780170229852

2 The following extracts have been taken from the accounting records of *Great Gardens* for the month of April 2019. The firm is registered for GST on the invoice basis.

GREAT GARDENS

Schedule of Accounts Receivable at 1 April

Spades Company	$667
Ready Rakes	1,380
Super Shovels	460
Weedfree	920
Pretty Plants	1,127
	$4,554

Sales journal summary, page 6

Date	No		Amount
Apr 6	351	Spades Company	$1,035
10	352	Ready Rakes	230
16	353	Super Shovels	460
22	354	Spades Company	207
24	356	Garden Gear	299
29	357	Pretty Plants	345
30	358	Super Shovels	368
			$2,944

Sales returns journal summary, page 1

Date	No		Amount
Apr 12	11	Ready Rakes	$ 69
15	12	Pretty Plants	23
30	13	Garden Gear	46
			$138

Cash receipts journal, page 4 (extract)

Date	Rec No		Cash	Discount allowed	GST on discount
Apr 19	865	Ready Rakes	1,311	60	9
20	866	Super Shovels	437	20	3
25	867	Spades Company	667	—	—
27	868	Pretty Plants	500	—	—

General Journal

Page 2

Date	Particulars	Dr $	Cr $
Apr 23	Accounts receivable – Spades Company	414	
	Consultancy fees		360
	GST payable		54
	(for consultancy fees charged to Spades Company, invoice 355)		
20	Accounts receivable – Super Shovels	276	
	Accounts receivable – Pretty Plants		276
	(to correct March posting error)		
30	Bad debts	800	
	GST payable	120	
	Accounts receivable – Weedfree		920
	(to write off Weedfree's account)		

DO THIS!

a Prepare the accounts receivable control account and subsidiary ledger for April 2019.
b Prepare a schedule of accounts receivable.

a
Great Gardens
General Ledger

Accounts receivable control	120

a

Great Gardens
Accounts Receivable Ledger

Spades Company	ARL1

Ready Rakes	ARL2

Super Shovels	ARL3

Weedfree	ARL4

Pretty Plants	ARL5

Accounting – A Next Step

ISBN: 9780170229852

Great Gardens
Accounts Receivable Ledger

Garden Gear	ARL6

b

Great Gardens
Schedule of Accounts Receivable as at 30 April 2019

DO THIS!

Answer the questions **c**, **d** and **e** below.

c Identify and describe the process that *Great Gardens* should have carried out before making the sale to *Garden Gear* on 24 April and explain why this process is necessary.

_____

_____

_____

_____

_____

d Examine the ledger account you prepared for *Weedfree*. Describe the event that has occurred and explain why this might have happened.

_____

_____

_____

_____

_____

e Examine the ledger account you prepared for *Pretty Plants*. Describe the events that have occurred. Use this information to suggest what *Great Gardens* could do to improve its credit policy and explain how your suggestion would help reduce future bad debts.

_____

_____

_____

_____

_____

_____

ISBN: 9780170229852

Accounts Receivable Subsystem

3 The balances of debtors' accounts in the accounts receivable ledger of *Robotix* at 30 September 2020 were as follows:

Debtor	Amount owing $	Age of account
Cheap Toys	8,900	current
Kids Galore	10,560	30 days
Playville	1,600	50% current 50% 30 days
Toys 'n More	4,740	50% current 25% 30 days 25% 60 days
Great Games	2,600	30% current 20% 30 days 20% 60 days 30% 4 months
Dressy Dolls	4,140	9 months

DO THIS!

Answer the questions below.

a Complete the aged accounts receivable report provided.

Robotix
Aged Accounts Receivable Report as at 30 September 2020

Age of account	Cheap Toys	Kids Galore	Playville	Toys 'n More	Great Games	Dressy Dolls	Total $	% of total
Current								
1 month								
2 months								
3 – 6 months								
Over 6 months								
Total								

b On 30 September, *Robotix* decided to write off all debts that are more than six months old. Prepare any general journal entries necessary to write off bad debts.

General Journal

Date	Particulars	Ref	Dr $	Cr $

c Use the information from the schedule you prepared in **a** above to comment on the credit collection efficiency of *Robotix* and explain the likely consequences.

_____
_____
_____
_____
_____
_____
_____

ISBN: 9780170229852

Customer Statements

The subsidiary ledger account for any particular debtor is used as the basis for the monthly statement. For example, the statement that *Kiri's Krafts* sent to *Kerikeri Store* at the end of September is shown below.

STATEMENT

Kiri's Krafts
458 Beach Road
Kerikeri
Telephone (09) 435-9857

Statement Date:	30 Sep 2019
Customer No:	10001
Due Date:	20 OCT 19
Balance: $	1,863.00

KERIKERI STORE
P O BOX 2587
KERIKERI

Total Amount Due (if paid after due date 20 Oct 2019) $1,863.00

Discounted Amount Due (if paid by due date 20 Oct 2019) $1,739.00

Please write in
amount paid $

Please detach top portion and enclose with your payment

- -

Date	Reference	Transaction Details	Dr	Cr	Balance
01 SEP		OPENING BALANCE			1,380.00
08 SEP	IN202	GOODS PURCHASED	1,725.00		3,105.00
16 SEP	IN206	GOODS PURCHASED	184.00		3,289.00
20 SEP	CN012	GOODS RETURNED		46.00	3,243.00
20 SEP	RT237	PAYMENT RECEIVED – THANK YOU		1,288.00	1,955.00
20 SEP	RT237	PROMPT PAYMENT DISCOUNT		92.00	1,863.00

Opening Balance	Interest	Purchases and Charges	Payments	Adjustments	Closing Balance
1,380.00	0.00	1,909.00 +	1,288.00 –	138.00 –	1,863.00

Current	Overdue 30 days	Overdue 60 days	Overdue 90 days and over	Finance Rate
1,863.00	0.00	0.00	0.00	19.5%

Phonix Print

Important!

- The top part of this statement is a **remittance advice**. If payment is made by cheque, this portion of the statement is returned by the customer with the cheque. Remittance advices are still included with statements even though electronic banking is now the most common from of payment.
- The due date for payment and the amounts due for payment before and after the discount date are in a prominent position.
- The customer number is the chart of accounts number in the accounts receivable ledger. *Kerikeri Store* was debtor number 1 in the ledger of *Kiri's Krafts*.

ISBN: 9780170229852

 PHOTOCOPYING PROHIBITED   **Accounts Receivable Subsystem**

- The reference column refers to the source documents which have been used to post the entries to *Kerikeri Store's* account. These reference numbers are the same as those which were found in the appropriate journals.
- The transaction details are shown from the point of view of the customer. For example, sales which were recorded on 8 September are shown in the customer's statement as goods purchased.
- The age of the account is shown at the bottom of the statement. There is a space which shows amounts that are overdue for 30 days, 60 days or 90 days and over. *Kerikeri Store* does not have an overdue account, hence zero balances are shown in these portions of the statement.
- It is compulsory in terms of the Credit Contracts Act 1981 for a finance rate to be shown on the statement where a customer is charged interest on any outstanding balance. In this instance the finance rate is shown at 19.5%.

The importance of statements

Sending regular statements to customers is an important part of the credit control process. Normal monthly credit terms require payment by the 20th of the month following the statement date. The statement above was issued on 30 September and is due for payment on 20 October.

A statement serves the following purposes:
- it provides a list of the customer's transactions for the month which the customer business can reconcile with its own records;
- it provides a summary of the amount owing at the end of the month and notifies the customer of the amount payable, the due date and any discounts that may be available; and
- it provides an opportunity to remind the customer about any amount that has been owing for more than the allowable credit period.

Some businesses require their customers to 'pay on invoice' which means that payment is due within a specified period of the invoice being issued. For example, many tradesmen (and some retailers) have a statement on their invoices such as *Payment due within 7 days*. Even in these cases, it is a good idea to send a statement at the end of the month because:
- it shows the customer business that its payment has (or has not) been received
- it reminds the customer that the business exists and may serve as a form of advertising
- it provides an opportunity to include other materials, such as advertising for new products or special announcements, in an indirect manner.

A business should not rely only on a monthly statement as the only means of chasing overdue accounts. Any missed payments require follow-up within a few days, using the processes described earlier. The ledger account for *Hikurangi House* on pages 46 and 47 shows a charge for interest because this account is overdue. *Kiri's Krafts* should have contacted *Hikurangi House* in late September, before issuing the statement at the end of the month.

ISBN: 9780170229852

Activities

1 Use the ledger account for *Rotorua Souvenirs* on page 46 or 47 to prepare the September statement issued by *Kiri's Krafts*. You should calculate prompt payment discounts at 5% and you may round to the nearest $.

STATEMENT

Kiri's Krafts
458 Beach Road
Kerikeri
Telephone (09) 435-9857

ROTORUA SOUVENIRS

P O BOX 23-156

ROTORUA

Statement Date:	
Customer No:	10002
Due Date:	
Amount Due: $	

Total Amount Due (if paid after due date 20 Oct 2019)2

Discounted Amount Due (if paid by due date 20 Oct 2019)

$	Please write in
$	amount paid $

Please detach top portion and enclose with your payment

- -

Date	Reference	Transaction Details	Dr	Cr	Balance

Opening Balance	Interest	Purchases and Charges	Payments	Adjustments	Total Due

Current	Overdue 30 days	Overdue 60 days	Overdue 90 days and over	Finance Rate
				19.5%

Phonix Print

Accounts Receivable Subsystem

ISBN: 9780170229852

2) Use the ledger account for *Te Anau Travel* on page 46 or 47 to prepare the September statement issued by *Kiri's Krafts*. You should calculate prompt payment discounts at 5% and you may round to the nearest $.

STATEMENT

Kiri's Krafts
458 Beach Road
Kerikeri
Telephone (09) 435-9857

TE ANAU TRAVEL	Statement Date: _____
P O BOX 21	Customer No: 10003
TE ANAU	Due Date: _____
	Amount Due: $ _____

Total Amount Due (if paid after due date 20 Oct 2019)2

Discounted Amount Due (if paid by due date 20 Oct 2019)

$	Please write in
$	amount paid $

Please detach top portion and enclose with your payment

- -

Date	Reference	Transaction Details	Dr	Cr	Balance

Opening Balance	Interest	Purchases and Charges	Payments	Adjustments	Total Due

Current	Overdue 30 days	Overdue 60 days	Overdue 90 days and over	Finance Rate
				19.5%

Phonix Print

Internal Control over Accounts Receivable

The main purposes of internal control over accounts receivable are:

- to ensure that goods are sold only to credit-worthy customers
- to ensure that all goods which leave the premises are correctly invoiced
- to ensure that all accounts are paid and that these payments are recorded accurately
- to ensure that credit notes are issued only for bona fide returns.

Document flowcharts

The document flowchart below represents one system of accounting for credit sales. This flowchart has been greatly simplified. Genuine document flowcharts show a good deal more detail than the one given. However, the flowchart is useful to show the movement of documents in the subsystem and the points where internal controls are applied.

Accounting – A Next Step
Accounts Receivable Subsystem

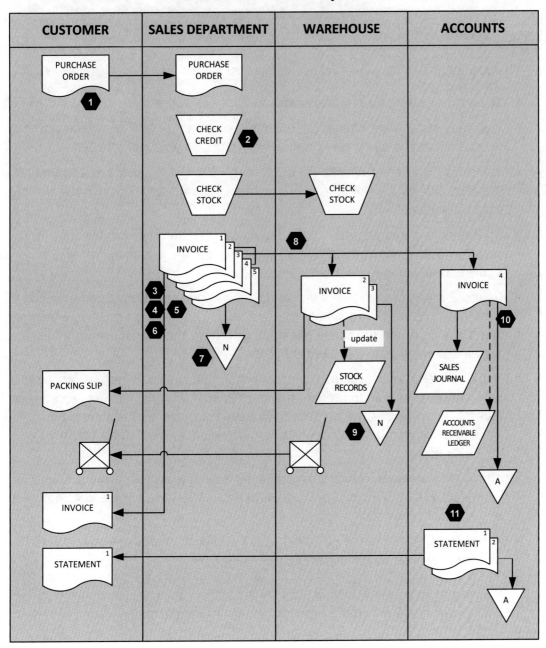

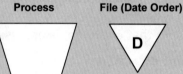

Guide to reading flowcharts

- The following symbols in the flowchart have special meanings:

Document	Accounting Record	Process	File (Date Order)
			D

- The flowchart is divided into separate departments. There is a separate column for each of: customer, sales, store (warehouse) and accounts. each column represents a separation, or different people involved in the sales process.
- The flowchart shows the earliest events at the top, with later events following in sequence down the page.
- The document is reproduced as it flows from one department to the next.
- The flowchart is prepared from the business point of view. Thus, all business documents are filed but filing for the customer is not shown.

The document flow for a manual accounts receivable subsystem is as follows:

- The customer sends a **purchase order** to the sales department.

- The sales department **checks** the customer's credit rating. If the credit rating is unsatisfactory the customer is notified and the sale does not proceed.

- The sales department **checks** the availability of stock. If stock is not available, the customer will be asked if he or she wishes to wait for stock to arrive or cancel the order.

- An **invoice** is **prepared** in the sales department. Four carbon copies are prepared at the same time. Copy 5 remains in the invoice book, forming a numerical file.

- Copies 2 and 3 of the invoice are **sent** to the warehouse. Copy 2 is enclosed with the goods which are **sent** to the customer. This copy is known as a **packing slip**. Copy 3 is used to **update the stock records** in the warehouse. It is then **filed** in the warehouse in numerical order.

- Copy 4 is sent to the accounts department so that the customer's records can be updated. It is used to prepare the **sales journal** and the **accounts receivable ledger**. These records will be used to **prepare** the customer's **statement** at the end of the month. The copy of the invoice is then **filed** alphabetically by customer name.

- The original **invoice** is **sent** to the customer as a request for payment. Some control should be built into the system to ensure that the invoice does not arrive before the goods.

- A **statement** is **sent** to the customer at the end of the month. A copy is **filed** in alphabetical order in the accounts department.

You should note that all documents are accounted for. They are either filed in various departments within the business or sent to the customer.

Internal control

Simple procedures together with the correct separation of duties can ensure that internal control is adequate. The position of each of the required internal controls is shown on the flowchart, and described below, together with its purpose.

Internal Control	Description	Purpose
1	Order taken by different person from the one who prepares the invoice.	Ensures all orders billed correctly. Prevent order-taker from discounting goods for friends.
2	Customer credit check	Prevents sale of goods to customers who may not pay.
3	Invoice forms prenumbered.	Prevents issue of false documents and removal of copies.
4	Customer order number shown on invoice	Ensures order is legitimate and customer intends to pay for goods.
5	Invoice prepared before goods leave premises.	Prevents goods being sent without being invoiced.
6	Quantities of goods entered on invoice by one person and calculations done by another.	Ensures correct prices are charged and not discounted to friends.
7	Copy 5 of invoice filed in sales department	Provides a complete record of authorised sales for goods to leave premises.
8	Invoice prepared by a different person (sales) from the one who sends the goods (store).	Prevents goods being sent (for example, to friends), without being invoiced or recorded.
9	Copy 3 of invoice filed in store	Provides record of authorisation for goods to leave store.
10	Copy 4 used by accounts to update sales journal and accounts receivable ledger.	Separation of duties prevents those making sale updating customer records.
11	Regular statements sent to customers.	Provides external check on recording procedures.

There are further internal controls relating to accounts receivable that have been covered in previous sections, but are not shown in the flowchart. Specifically, these relate to the issue of credit notes and the receipt of cash from customers.

Credit notes

Description	Purpose
Credit note forms prenumbered.	Prevents issue of false documents and removal of copies.
Original invoice number shown on invoice	Ensures goods were purchased from the business in the first instance (and not from elsewhere).
Goods returned physically inspected and counted	Ensures the correct quantity has been returned and goods are fit for resale, unless they are being returned due to damage in which case the damage can be assessed.
Authorised by senior member of staff	Ensures credit note issued for bona fide returns

Cash receipts

Description	Purpose
Separation of recording cash receipts from updating customer records	Prevents crediting customer accounts when no payment actually received.
Separation of recording cash receipts from issuing credit notes	Prevents issuing credit notes to cover for stolen cash.

Activities

1 Describe internal controls that could be introduced to prevent the following events from taking place:

a the sale of goods to a customer whose accounts was recently written off as a bad debt

_____

_____

_____

_____

b i the false invoicing of goods to a business

_____

_____

_____

_____

ii the interception of the payment when it is received in the mail

_____

_____

_____

_____

c the issue of a credit note to a customer who has not actually returned any goods.

_____

_____

_____

_____

d theft of goods by warehouse staff who claim they have been sent to a customer.

_____

_____

_____

_____

e an error in posting an invoice amount to a customer's account in the accounts receivable ledger, such as posting $450 instead of $540.

_____

_____

_____

_____

The documents below represent the transactions of *Hobbies 'n Handcrafts* for the month of April 2019.

TAX INVOICE No: 451
8 April 2019

Hobbies 'n Handcrafts
INVOICE
GST No: 84-957-582

TO: Raging Rugs

FOR:	Rug wool	$3,105.00
Total (incl GST)		$3,105.00

TAX INVOICE No: 452
14 April 2019

Hobbies 'n Handcrafts
INVOICE
GST No: 84-957-582

TO: Pins 'n Needles

FOR:	Fabric	$4,140.00
	Freight	23.00
Total (incl GST)		$4,163.00

TAX INVOICE No: 453
16 April 2019

Hobbies 'n Handcrafts
INVOICE
GST No: 84-957-582

TO: Wild Wools

FOR:	Yarn	$2,070.00
	Freight	46.00
Total (incl GST)		$2,116.00

TAX INVOICE No: 454
25 April 2019

Hobbies 'n Handcrafts
INVOICE
GST No: 84-957-582

TO: Wild Wools

FOR:	Canvas	$1,380.00
	Rug hooks	690.00
Total (incl GST)		$2,070.00

TAX INVOICE No: 455
30 April 2019

Hobbies 'n Handcrafts
INVOICE
GST No: 84-957-582

TO: Fancy Dress

FOR:	Lace	$920.00
	Buttons	115.00
Total (incl GST)		$1,035.00

TAX INVOICE No: 023
Inv Ref: 452   18 April 2019

Hobbies 'n Handcrafts
CREDIT NOTE
GST No: 84-957-582

TO: Pins 'n Needles

FOR:	Fabric	
Total (incl GST)		$529.00

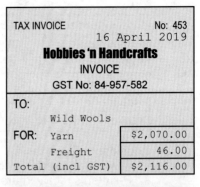

TAX INVOICE No: 024
Inv Ref: 453   29 April 2019

Hobbies 'n Handcrafts
CREDIT NOTE
GST No: 84-957-582

TO: Wild Wools

FOR:	Yarn	
Total (incl GST)		$322.00

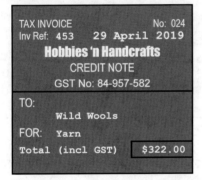

No: 309
7 April 2019

Hobbies 'n Handcrafts
RECEIPT
GST No: 84-957-582

TO: Wild Wools

FOR:	March account	
		$1,380.00

No: 310
10 April 2019

Hobbies 'n Handcrafts
RECEIPT
GST No: 84-957-582

TO: Raging Rugs

FOR:	March account	
		$2,277.00

(discount $253.00)

No: 311
15 April 2019

Hobbies 'n Handcrafts
RECEIPT
GST No: 84-957-582

FROM: Fancy Dress

FOR:	March account	
Amount paid		$575.00

MEMORANDUM

Hobbies 'n Handcrafts

DATE: *10 April 2019*

Wild Wools called. Need credit of $690 wrongly charged last month. Invoice 448 should have been charged to Raging Rugs.

MEMORANDUM

Hobbies 'n Handcrafts

DATE: *11 April 2019*

Need to give 10% discount to Wild Wools on last month's account after correction of error in statement. They have already paid so credit against this month's account.

MEMORANDUM

Hobbies 'n Handcrafts

DATE: *30 April 2019*

Received notice from Official Assignee. Owner of Threadz is bankrupt. Need to write this account off.

OurBank

STATEMENT

30 APR 2019

Date	Particulars	Dr/Cr
APR 19	PINS 'N NEEDLES	$1,800.00 DR

Details of accounts receivable at 1 April 2019 are:

	Total	Current	1 month	2 months	3 months	> 3 months
Pins 'n Needles	4,945	2,967	1,978			
Raging Rugs	2,530	2,530				
Fancy Dress	1,495	897	299	299		
Wild Wools	2,070	2,070				
Threadz	920					920
TOTAL	11,960	8,464	2,277	299	–	920

Additional information
- The firm is registered for GST on the invoice basis.
- Payments received are applied to the oldest debt first.
- Discount of 10% is allowed if an account is paid in full by the 20th of the following month.
- Cost of goods sold is 60% of the GST exclusive sale price.

Hobbies 'n Handcrafts

DO THIS!

a Record the transactions from the documents in the journals below. Posting references are required for the **accounts receivable** ledger only.
b Prepare the accounts receivable control account and subsidiary ledger for April 2019.
c Prepare an aged accounts receivable report as at 30 April 2019.

a

Hobbies 'n Handcrafts
Sales Journal   **Page 7**

		Inv no	Ref	Total $	Sales $	Freight $	GST payable $	Cost of goods sold $

Hobbies 'n Handcrafts
Sales Returns and Allowances Journal   **Page 1**

		C/N no	Ref	Total $	Sales returns & allowances $	GST payable $	Cost of goods sold $

Accounting – A Next Step

PHOTOCOPYING PROHIBITED

ISBN: 9780170229852

Hobbies 'n Handcrafts
Cash Receipts Journal (extract)

		Rec no	Ref	Discount allowed $	GST on discount $	Cash $	Accounts receivable $

Hobbies 'n Handcrafts
General Journal

Date	Particulars	Ref	Dr $	Cr $

b

Hobbies 'n Handcrafts
General Ledger

Accounts receivable control	120

b

Hobbies 'n Handcrafts
Accounts Receivable Ledger

Pins 'n Needles	ARL1

Raging Rugs	ARL2

Fancy Dress	ARL3

Wild Wools	ARL4

Threadz	ARL5

Accounting – A Next Step

ISBN: 9780170229852

c

Hobbies 'n Handcrafts
Aged Accounts Receivable Report as at 30 April 2019

Age of account	Pins 'n Needles	Raging Rugs	Fancy Dress	Wild Wools	Threadz	Total $	% of total
Current							
1 month							
2 months							
3 months							
Over 3 months							
Total							

PART B

Hobbies 'n Handcrafts is a wholesale firm owned by Harriet Harris. Harriet runs the business herself, with the help of Tania, who works full-time, and Anna, who works part-time as required.

Harriet is often overseas sourcing new products. Recently she has been away more often because she wants to expand the business by setting up an online store to sell goods to the public. This year she was away for most of April and did not return until early May.

Tania is primarily responsible for filling orders as they come in through the firm's website. When an order is received, she picks the goods from the shelves and uses an invoicing software package to create an invoice and enter the quantity of goods sold. She prints one copy as a packing slip which she sends to the customer with the goods. At the end of each week, Harriet enters the prices, GST and totals on the invoices and emails a copy to the customer. If Harriet is away, Anna completes the invoices and emails them whenever she has time.

While Harriet is away, Tania runs the business. Anna works extra hours during these periods. She helps Tania by picking the goods from the shelves after Tania has prepared the packing slip.

Harriet normally deals with returned goods and the issue of credit notes herself. She prepares the credit notes using the same software package and emails them to the customers. If Harriet is away, Tania deals with the returns and enters quantities on the credit notes. Anna uses the latest catalogue price to complete and email credit notes when she does the invoices.

The general ledger is maintained by a business management firm that clears the mail, does the banking, issues receipts where necessary and reconciles the bank statements. This firm sends Harriet a daily report showing all payments received from customers and Harriet enters this information into the accounts receivable ledger on the software. If Harriet is away, she uses her laptop to enter the information so that the ledger is always up to date. At the end of each month, Harriet sends this firm the totals of invoices and credit notes issued during the month so they can send her the balance of the accounts receivable control account to use for her reconciliation.

At the end of the month, the software package outputs the customer statements and the accounts receivable ledger. Harriet then reconciles the accounts receivable ledger and the accounts receivable control account before sending the statements to the customers. Harriet always makes sure that she does this work herself and times her travels so that she is back in time to do it each month.

Harriet has monitored credit sales herself in the past, but is concerned that her increasing absences from the business are resulting in less efficient credit control. When she returned in the first week of May, she was very upset to find that a sale of $10,000 had been made to *Threadz* on 2 May and that significant sales had been made to new customers in the previous few days.

DO THIS!

Answer the questions **a** to **e** overleaf.

ISBN: 9780170229852

Accounts Receivable Subsystem

a Explain the purpose of the aged accounts receivable report and how Harriet might use it to improve the cash flow of *Hobbies 'n Handcrafts*.

_____

_____

_____

_____

_____

_____

_____

_____

_____

_____

_____

b Harriet cannot understand how the error in posting *Wild Wools'* account was not discovered when she reconciled the accounts receivable control account with the accounts receivable ledger at the end of March.

  i Explain the purpose of this reconciliation.

_____

_____

_____

_____

_____

  ii Explain why the error was not discovered during the reconciliation process.

_____

_____

_____

_____

_____

_____

c *Fancy Dress* complained that they received an invoice dated 30 April which appeared on their April statement, but they did not receive the goods until 3 May. Explain how this might have happened and suggest how such events could be prevented in future.

_____

_____

_____

_____

_____

_____

_____

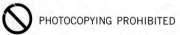

ISBN: 9780170229852